PRESERVING THE WEST

California

Arizona

Nevada

Utah

Idaho

Oregon

Washington

RANDOLPH DELAHANTY

Photographs by
E. ANDREW McKINNEY

Additional photographs by
RANDOLPH LANGENBACH

Foreword by WILLIAM T. FRAZIER,
National Trust for Historic Preservation

PANTHEON BOOKS
New York

For Elias and Irma Delehanty

(Frontispiece): The 1892 Public School No. 1 in Silver City, Idaho, is preserved by the Owyhee County Cattlemen's Association as a meeting hall. Upstairs is a private museum assembled by the county's dedicated local historian, Mildretta Adams.

Library of Congress Cataloging in Publication Data

Delahanty, Randolph.
    Preserving the West.

    1. Historic sites—West (U.S.)—Conservation and preservation—Addresses, essays, lectures. 2. Architecture—West (U.S.)—Conservation and preservation—Addresses, essays, lectures. 3. West (U.S.)—History, Local—Addresses, essays, lectures. I. McKinney, E. Andrew. II. National Trust for Historic Preservation in the United States. III. Title.
F595.3.D44 1985   978   84-26584
ISBN 0-394-52770-4
ISBN 0-394-74070-X

PRESERVING THE WEST

CONTENTS

FOREWORD

WHAT ARE the unique characteristics of the American West that have defined, and sometimes constrained, historic preservation? First, its geography—the vast expanses of land, the rugged terrain, the remote settlements—has limited contact between communities. Likewise, the climatic extremes and recurrent earthquakes have destroyed many early structures, most of which were built in a hurry and were fragile. Those that remain are neither as old nor as elaborate as the earliest examples in the East, and many people perceive them as unworthy of preservation. One often finds that the oldest buildings are the hardest to preserve, because communities want to replace these humble structures with "modern" and "progressive" architecture.

As *Preserving the West* shows, federal ownership of millions of acres of land in the region has made the federal government a prime actor in historic preservation. Because many of these lands also contain prehistoric sites, archeological concerns are more prominent than in other areas of the United States. But the boom-and-bust cycles in mining, lumbering, agriculture, public works, and now tourism cause continuing threats to the historic fabric of the West.

The preservationist's case is made all the more difficult by the independent attitude of the Westerner, and by the region's strong tradition of property rights. In view of the antiregulatory sentiment that prevails, it is ironic that Westerners have passed some of the strongest state environmental protection laws in the country. Perhaps the scale and splendor of the West's natural beauty dwarf the importance people place on the built environment.

Despite these factors, the West still has an important history of preservation activities. At the turn of this century in California, the Historical Landmarks Committee of the Native Sons of the American West, led by Joseph Knowland, worked to save many of the historic missions and adobe structures of the West. In 1928 Knowland also acted as historical adviser to the California State Park Survey supervised by Frederick Law Olmsted. Its listing of historic sites ran to more than fifty pages, at the time one of the most extensive surveys in the nation.

Mining towns and places evoking images of the "Wild West" also captivated preservationists' interests. In the 1930s both Tombstone, Arizona and Columbia, California attempted, with limited success, to develop tourist-oriented preservation programs based on their rich past. An especially early example of community-wide interest in preservation occurred in Monterey, California, where the city fathers passed a historic preservation master plan and related zoning ordinance in 1939, at a time when only a handful of Eastern cities—for example, Charleston and New Orleans—were passing similar laws. (For the reader interested in more information about Western preservation activities over time,

Charles Hosmer's *Presence of the Past* and *Preservation Comes of Age* are the two primers in the field.)

Today, preservation in the West reflects changes in the preservation movement nationwide. Turning old buildings to new commercial uses is an effort supported by federal tax incentives. In addition, the neighborhood-conservation movement is particularly strong throughout the West's urban areas. New bed-and-breakfast inns are continually opening in historic buildings in countless smaller communities. Main streets of towns in every state in the region are reusing their historic commercial buildings to bring new life to downtown shopping areas.

At the same time, old inner-city hotels are being restored to house residents of low and moderate income. In several of our Western cities, high-rise structures are no longer quite so high, and their designs are noticeably more sympathetic to their historic neighbors. Interest in the rich maritime history of the Pacific Coast continues to increase, while archeological laws are being strengthened in the Southwest to protect Indian sites.

Local programs are active; many communities in the West are establishing historic commissions to survey, identify, and protect their local landmarks. Furthermore, six states have set up private organizations to coordinate and promote the important preservation activities in all of their cities and counties (see Regional Source Guide at the end of the book).

It is easy to lament the historical and architectural losses that the West has suffered, but one must not forget the uniquely independent spirit of the Westerner. Western preservation is a relatively young enterprise; the movement must continue to mature, as it has already done in many other sections of the country.

Nevertheless, as *Preserving the West* shows so graphically, there is progress to report in the region. More and more, Westerners are committed to studying their past and to mobilizing their neighbors and friends. In the process they are gaining more public support, which is absolutely essential for the development of a strong preservation ethic.

"Speaking of old buildings," John Ruskin said in his *Seven Lamps of Architecture,* "they are not just ours. They partly belong to those who built them and partly to all generations of mankind who are to follow us. . . . What other men gave their strength and wealth and life to accomplish . . . belongs to all their successors." This impassioned plea for the public stewardship of our historic buildings may not yet be felt in the American West as strongly as Ruskin would have liked, but there is every sign that we are getting closer to that ideal. If Randolph Delahanty's work prompts more discussion of that ethic, then we will all be the richer for it.

WILLIAM T. FRAZIER
Director, Western Regional Office
National Trust for Historic Preservation

AUTHOR'S NOTE

THIS BOOK is one observer's view of a vast and varied landscape, but it has had the benefit of many other people's expertise. I began my research with a list of questions addressed to the knowledgeable staff of the Western Regional Office of the National Trust for Historic Preservation in San Francisco, and to its former head, John L. Frisbee III. I was seeking projects that epitomized not only preservation but the history of each state, region, or city as well. With this "menu" I then interviewed by telephone each State Historic Preservation Officer or staff historian in order to check my list, secure the names of people and preservation groups to contact in different localities, and winnow out an itinerary of places to visit. Once I had read as much as I could find on my list of likely sites, E. Andrew McKinney and I planned a series of loops through various parts of the West and set out by auto to study and photograph the places in this book. As we traveled I refined my list of sites and added several that are not being preserved but deserve to be.

My next step was to send each chapter to a local expert for correction. In Arizona I wish to thank Professor Robert Giebner; in San Francisco, H. Grant DeHart; at Stanford University, Robert Nerrie; in Santa Barbara, John C. Woodward; in Los Angeles, Ruthann Lerner; in San Diego, Ronald A. Smith; in Utah, Martin Kilson, Tom Carter, and Mayor Craig Paulson; in Idaho, Ed Jagels; in Oregon, Robertson Collins, Richard H. Engman, and David Powers; in Washington State, David M. Hansen; in Tacoma, Patricia Sias; in Seattle, Harriet Sherburne; and in Spokane, Janice Rutherford. For looking over the entire text I wish to thank William T. Frazier, Director, and the staff of the Western Regional Office of the National Trust for Historic Preservation in San Francisco, as well as Diane Maddex, editor of Preservation Press books for the National Trust. It was her idea to develop a series of books, of which this is the first, documenting preservation in the regions of the United States. The Trust's helpfulness has preserved me from many errors; those that remain are my own. The selection and interpretation of places are mine and not necessarily those of the National Trust for Historic Preservation, the various State Offices of Historic Preservation, or those individuals and local preservation organizations mentioned in the text.

Finally, I wish to acknowledge my great debt to E. Andrew McKinney, whose photographs fill most of this book, and to Randolph Langenbach, who photographed Stanford University. Andrew's good humor, expert driving, quick and professional work, and strong coffee, brewed in motels and out on the open range, fueled this project. I am happy to thank him for both his photography and his friendship.

RANDOLPH DELAHANTY
January 1985

A WESTERN PANORAMA

This simple, frame, Western false-front post office in Tropic, Utah, was made obsolete by a new building facing the highway. This Mormon town preserved it near the village green.

THIS BOOK aims to convey a panoramic view of the current state of architectural and landscape preservation in the American West, a huge and dynamic region. Needless to say, this is a select view; not everything is, or could be, included. I have sought to present preservation successes, and a few failures as well, that typify the architectural and historical variety of the West. For there is not one West, but rather several distinct Wests. The Hollywood image of the wooden cowboy town is not *the* West, but only a part of a much more complex and architecturally rich region.

A Western Preservation Itinerary

After a brief photographic overture included in this part, the book begins with the preservation achievements of the Navajos in the Monument Valley Tribal Park in northern Arizona, where an entire landscape, including traditionally dispersed hogans, has been maintained intact. A second great preservation success in Arizona is in the far south of the state, where Mission San Xavier del Bac, the greatest Spanish colonial architectural work in the United States, has been kept alive by the vibrant piety of the Papago people on the San Xavier Indian Reservation.

The modest adobe barrios of Tucson, another example of community preservation, show in their architecture the fusion of Mexican and Anglo culture

in this part of the Southwest. An examination of the exceptionally well-designed mining town of Ajo completes this brief view of Arizona.

The preservation story of San Francisco, whose initial wealth was based on the mines of the interior, begins the California story. Historically the sophisticated metropolis of the nineteenth-century West, San Francisco is now a place where preservation is nearly automatic in the Victorian neighborhoods and

When this northern Nevada ranch built a modern one-story house nearby, the old board-and-batten two-story homestead was closed up but not demolished. Preservation is keeping links with the past.

Falling gently into ruin, this eastern Washington hay and mule barn has no economic use now that tractors have replaced the animal teams of the past. Farmers hold on to their barns, but every winter takes its toll.

where imaginative preservation efforts are being made in the booming high-rise downtown. The love for old domestic architecture in San Francisco is so deeply ingrained that truly heroic and very expensive rescue operations have been conducted on many buildings it would have been more economical to tear down. Most of this preservation activity has been individual and spontaneous and not dependent on city or federal subsidy, or even on local preservation organizations. However, the rich early-twentieth-century Victorian heritage downtown faces genuine difficulties, and the current "solution" of partial or façade preservation is raising real problems for those concerned with the city's architectural heritage.

From San Francisco our view shifts south, first to nearby Stanford University, endowed with the wealth of the transcontinental railroad and one of the great landscape and architectural creations in the West. Here California's most serious preservation challenge—earthquakes—is being successfully met in the faithful rebuilding of the fine century-old masonry structures surrounding the Old Quad. Farther south is Santa Barbara, where the coordinated rebuilding after the great quake of 1924 resulted in an outstandingly coherent cityscape and the creation of a "Santa Barbara style." One of the West's most effective efforts at design control in designated historic districts is preserving Santa Barbara's urban form while encouraging sympathetic and creative new works.

We continue south to Los Angeles, since the 1920s the most important economic and cultural center in the West, with an outstanding heritage of early modern design of international significance. Its great boom periods, the teens, twenties, and thirties, are now long enough past to be considered historic. In Los Angeles, preservation is beginning to seep into public consciousness as the city achieves cultural maturity. On the level of private property, enough Angelenos are taking an interest in their stylistic heritage—mission, Art Deco, and Moderne—to make a noticeable difference. But the story in Los Angeles is mixed; the city and county governments in particular have a long way to go in understanding the value of preserving their fine public buildings. The Los Angeles Public Library downtown, one of the finest buildings in the West, is only now getting the appreciation it merits.

South of Los Angeles is San Diego, now California's second most populous city, where economic growth and political leadership have encouraged the preservation of the historic Stingaree red-light district as the born-again Gaslamp Quarter. Nevertheless, auto-oriented shopping and recreation patterns persist here, showing how difficult inner-city preservation is when people prefer the suburbs to the historic core.

From California we move to central Nevada and the historic red-brick mining town of Austin, dead center in the sagebrush West. Here two great preservation realities are seen at their starkest: the impor-

This pioneer log cabin in a backyard in Spring City, Utah, has been a house, a storage shed, and a playhouse called the Long Branch. Now that the children have grown, it is one man's small museum housing antique furniture, happy memories, and such infrequently used items as an ice-cream maker.

The same man preserves an old lambing shed on his property. New partitions have been inserted but all the pioneer timbers have been preserved in a still-living building.

tance of healthy economic activity (which is concentrated in modern Nevada at the gambling towns along the borders) and the destructiveness that goes along with this state's ethos of near-anarchic individualism. (Nevada is the Western state least respectful of either its historic buildings or its land. One sad detail says it all: in Nevada most traffic signs and historical markers are used repeatedly as targets.) The fate of one anonymous ranch in far northern Humboldt County again shows that a healthy economy is the indispensable foundation of architectural preservation.

From Nevada we move deeper into the heart of the Great Basin and to the unique landscape, town-building, and architectural achievement of the Mormons. The most important communalists in the highly individualistic West, the Latter-Day Saints built "nucleated villages" in their remote Zion rather than the isolated farmsteads traditional in America. But Mormon society is changing rapidly, and though one might think that a society so concerned with genealogy would also treasure its historic rural villages, preservation is emerging only slowly in Utah. A string of Mormon-designed towns *does* survive in Mormondom's heartland, but much more awareness of their great value is needed. Spring City in Sanpete County, south of booming, rebuilding, self-destructing Salt Lake City, is perhaps the best of these surviving Zions; preservation has taken root there and promises to succeed. In Salt Lake City itself, isolated monuments such as the famous Mormon Temple have been preserved, and some neighborhoods, especially near the state capitol and the university, are strongly preservationist, but commercial and even church treasures continue to be lost.

Idaho, like Nevada, has always been a relatively poor state. The riches from her mines built solid architecture in Spokane, Washington, but very little great architecture in the state itself. And yet there is one outstanding preservation story in the state: Silver City, once an almost-abandoned wooden mining town preserved in the first place by its remoteness and now by the intense love of many Idahoans and other Westerners, from the one man who stayed in town during the nadir of the wartime 1940s to all the Masonic lodges of Idaho and from the Roman Catholic Diocese of Boise to the Owyhee County Cattlemen's Association. Silver City is one of the most evocative relics of the Old West. In a region where fake "Old West" seems inexorably to replace real local

history (covering over historic stone buildings with cowboy-Western weathered boards, for example), Silver City, Idaho, is the real thing.

Jacksonville, Oregon, another former mining town —this one built of brick, not wood—has a different but equally encouraging preservation story to tell. In an effort involving everyone from the town's homeowners to the local preservation-minded bank, the phone company, and the post office, Jacksonville first rescued itself and then, more amazingly, accommodated itself to tourism without destroying the historic charm that brings people there in the first place.

In Portland, Oregon's metropolis, preservation in the historic downtown districts must knit back together the old sections of a city that virtually obliterated its important cast-iron heritage and that now faces the difficult design problem of building appropriately on the parking lots that scar its historic areas. Portland is making important strides in this process of "in-fill" construction. Happily, outside Portland, the nearby Columbia River Scenic Highway, Multnomah Falls Lodge, and Timberline Lodge on Mount Hood, superb and early examples of auto-oriented design, are being actively preserved.

Turning north, the preservation story in Washington State is one of the happiest of all. Historically not one of the richest parts of the West, nor the first to see the very beginnings of preservation (that honor belongs to California), it nonetheless is a leader in the

This simple but effective frame church in Battle Mountain, Nevada, has been preserved by the two congregations that share it, St. Andrew's Episcopal Church and Christ Lutheran Church.

These fine Victorian red-brick commercial buildings in Austin, Nevada, illustrate the importance of a solid economic base to preservation: Because no significant new activity has replaced the closed mines in the area, poverty both preserves and slowly destroys this rare survivor from the Old West.

region in keeping its old cities and neighborhoods alive and attractive and in maintaining high standards at its many landmarks, state parks, and other public places. Seattle on Puget Sound, and Spokane deep in the far eastern wheat belt, stand out especially in this regard. In these two commercial cities the downtown districts are flourishing and vintage buildings are being restored as new buildings go up around them. Tacoma, the state's principal old industrial city, has also emerged as a preservation-minded place. Even Washington State's small-town main streets have begun to show an interest in working with, rather than against, their nineteenth-century architectural heritage. From the tiny hamlet of Oysterville on the coast to its major urban areas, Washington State shows how imaginative historic preser-

vation contributes to the livability of a place.

It's a long way from central Nevada to coastal Seattle, and as you will see in these photo essays, the distance is measured in more than miles.

The Many Wests

The Federal West

One other vast "state" in the West needs to be mentioned: the enormous federal domain of some 738 million acres, about one-third of the region. In Nevada 86.1 percent of the state is federally owned and administered by civil or military agencies. Even in California, settled earlier than its neighbors, 45.3 percent of the state is federal property. When one

The main street in Grants Pass, Oregon, is an extreme example of what has happened in many Western cities: the loss of good old architecture through drastic "improvements."

adds to this the state government's own land, county lands and buildings, and municipal real estate and parks, the startling fact emerges that most of California is publicly owned. Much of this land is unbuildable (the Sierras, for example), but the fact remains that important elements of the West's architectural heritage, from ancient ruins to military architecture, are owned by the nation as a whole.

Information gathered during scientific expeditions was initially responsible for the decision to take the Southwest's prehistoric ruins out of the pool of lands available for private appropriation. This was the single most important cultural preservation decision in the region's history. President Theodore Roosevelt's administrations (1901–1909) mark the critical turning point in federal attitudes toward the vast western public domain. The Antiquities Act of 1906, written to protect the Southwest's ancient sites, was the first piece of preservation legislation in the United States' history.

Coast and Interior, Rich and Poor

In the Far Western states, the Pacific coastal areas were the earliest to be settled by United States citizens, beginning in the 1830s. Oregon's Willamette Valley and coastal California were the first places to draw Yankee settlers, who initially came by ship. Later, the West's port cities—Portland, San Francisco, and Seattle—drew the mining and agricultural wealth of the developing interior to themselves. For example, the silver from under Virginia City,

The fine 1904 street clock of J. Jessop & Sons Jewelers in San Diego epitomizes the joy that preservation can add to the environment. Its shiny mechanism ticks away the years and links the city with its history.

Not everything that calls itself preservation is preservation. Moved to Heritage Square near San Diego's Old Town and turned into boutiques and offices, this 1880s Eastlake house has been put in a "history ghetto" and has lost its original associations with the city.

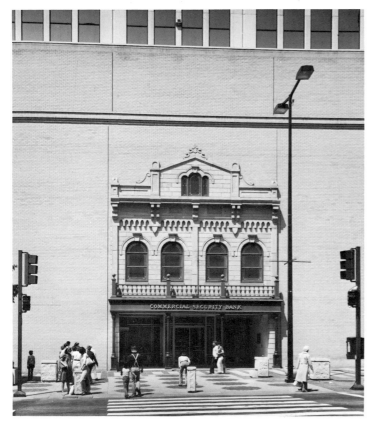

Partial preservation of façades can make a mockery of preservation. Here a fine stone façade from a jeweler's in Salt Lake City has been incongrously stuck onto the blank wall of a shopping center.

Nevada, helped pay for the lavish gingerbread of Victorian San Francisco, and the wheat from the fertile Willamette Valley created fine cast-iron-front commercial buildings in Portland. As the West developed during the last third of the nineteenth century, it was usually the city dwellers in these favored metropolises who were the first to support both natural conservation and later historic preservation. In the 1880s money went out from San Francisco to put roofs over the crumbling adobe ruins of Mission Carmel and other decaying monuments from the region's Spanish colonial past.

The coastal areas have continued to be the most culturally advanced parts of the West. When historic preservation first became a popular movement in the early 1970s, the coastal cities (along with inland Spokane, Washington) were again in the forefront in adopting a preservationist attitude toward man-made things: monuments, buildings, neighborhoods, and even industrial structures. Preservation today is especially strong in the strip from Santa Barbara, California, north to Seattle, Washington. Neighborhood organizations and citywide preservation groups are numerous there, and local and state political structures are often protective of the built environment.

Throwaway Cities and the Disposable Landscape: The Ghost Town

Exploited areas, especially mining regions but also some agricultural and ranching lands, have suffered a fate different from that of the wealthier coastal cities. Sudden building booms have usually been followed by sharp busts. Rough towns with a streak of opulence, the West's mining towns sprang up in the middle of nowhere, became immensely rich, and then withered away or disappeared completely when the mines gave out, banks failed, or prices shifted in the international metals market. Whereas New England and Ohio gave the nation an undying image of the village built around a common and the Deep South an image of the white-pillared plantation house, the West's contribution to the national mental landscape has been the ghost town—a string of places exploited and then abandoned when the main chance moved on somewhere else.

The West shows very clearly that building and rebuilding in the United States have not occurred slowly and steadily, but rather in a jerky series of wild expansions followed by sharp busts and, in unlucky regions, permanent depression or even complete obliteration. Even the metropolises rich enough to conserve their finest buildings have not always done so. Both Portland and Salt Lake City—each its state's major city, neither poor—have ravaged their architectural heritage. Los Angeles, the wealthiest and most creative city in the West since the 1920s, has been slow to recognize the importance of preserving as well as creating. Scanning the West, one finds that financial stability is only the beginning (if an essential beginning) for preservation; there must be the mentality and the will as well as the means.

National Development Patterns and Preservation

Preservation in the West is part of larger patterns of national development and redevelopment. At the center of most large American cities is the high-rise core of banks and office buildings (usually alongside, not in, the old streetcar-era downtown). These new downtowns, generally built after 1960, continue to expand. In the 1980s new, enclosed, luxury shopping "gallerias" began to spring up, also near rather than within the now usually blue-collar old downtown. Around this recent growth and its attendant backwash of parking lots is a ring of late-nineteenth-century and early-twentieth-century buildings where the poor, especially new immigrants, live. Beyond this wide gray zone with its pockets of gentrified nineteenth-century town houses is the outer ring of middle-class suburbs built from the 1920s through the early 1960s. These politically independent communities are physically stable though their population is aging. Circumscribing these settled, leafy towns is a wide new ring that continues to boom with industrial parks, shopping centers, and, increasingly, cluster housing densely arranged in disconnected developments linked to the highways, not to each other. This outer ring (along with the poor inner zone near the old downtown) houses most of the young families and children. And beyond these urbanized area's are the West's famous "wide open spaces": the seeming limitless ranching and farming country.

Big-City Downtowns: From Decay to Malls to Partial Preservation

In the new high-rise downtowns, preservation of older buildings has until recently faced impossible odds. Most Western downtowns shifted their focus between 1900 and 1960, discarding their old cores. Downtown San Diego's marked migration from Fifth Avenue across Broadway to C Street is a prime example; Seattle's shift north from Pioneer Square is another. These shifts both preserved and destroyed. The old streetcar-era downtowns were preserved by being passed over; they then became shopping and service districts for the poorest members of society (Los Angeles' Broadway is the classic example). Generally, the new high-rise downtowns also destroyed the older buildings in their path. Usually this development has moved relentlessly in one direction, toward the freeway or interstate highway: east in San Francisco, south in Portland, west in Los Angeles.

Once the old streetcar-era downtown was virtually comatose, cities became alarmed at the rot at their

Occasionally "preservation" actually destroys real history. At Mission San Jose near Fremont, California, a hundred-year-old Victorian church, St. Joseph's, was torn from its foundations in order to be able to build a so-called replica of the undistinguished adobe mission that once stood there.

Fortunately there has been real and imaginative preservation in the West. Ghirardelli Square in San Francisco, opened in 1964 and one of the first adaptive reuse projects in the nation, showed what could be done by combining old and new. Fine old buildings were preserved and adapted, with compatible modern buildings mixed in among them.

historic cores and decided to "do something." That "something" was almost never limiting the expansion at the edges, but rather making drastic physical changes in the old downtown. Turning Main Street into a mall—and tearing down the commercial and residential buildings in the flanking blocks for parking lots in order to make the downtown into an approximation of a suburban shopping center—was the usual "solution." Large and small cities followed this pattern during the 1960s; Yuma, Arizona, stands as the ultimate monument to this particular folly.

As it turned out, the downtown mall was not the answer to the revitalization of the old downtown, basically because malls hide shops from auto-encased shoppers and prevent impulse buying. Nor was the shape of the old downtown the basic problem, even if parking was. It was the booming of the edges that caused the death of the core. Cities such as Santa Barbara, which did not "mall" its main street, have fared much better than those such as Sacramento, which did. (Today Sacramento plans to tear out its 1960s mall and make its main shopping street a street again.) In Tacoma an effort is now being made to resuscitate a stillborn 1960s main-street mall with a mixture of preservation, adaptive reuse, and new high-rise construction. The idea there is to build a huge new tower hotel and a huge ugly parking structure, to preserve several old buildings in an interesting new pastiche, and to restore a fine 1918 movie palace at one end of the mall and convert it into a

One of the best things happening in contemporary preservation in the West is the restoration and rebirth of old hotels in small towns, as well as the creation of bed-and-breakfast inns in large, otherwise uneconomic houses. Here the 1891 Palace Hotel in rural Ukiah, California, has been carefully restored. Layers of the building's history, such as the 1940s maroon splash tiles beneath the windows, have been respected.

Urban preservation often involves adaptation to new conditions as well as restoration. The architect who restored Irving Gill's fine Horatio West Court of 1919 in Santa Monica, California, added a simple and appropriate apple-green fence that enhances the court's privacy and security yet looks like part of the original design.

municipal performing-arts hall. It is hoped that the now-completed hall will bring people—and life—downtown in the evenings.

Since about 1980, architectural preservation has begun to score a few complete and partial successes in historic downtowns. Today if a building of outstanding quality is publicly owned, it is unlikely to be demolished. If it is privately owned, it is increasingly likely to be "partially preserved"—that is, some part or ornament will probably be incorporated into a new building on the site. Often this is "preservation" as a sop to public opinion and to the planning commissions that must give approval to new construction proposals.

The long-fought battle to preserve the turn-of-the-century City of Paris department store in San Francisco is the classic example of this new twist. Sitting on what was and still is the best luxury retail corner in San Francisco, the *belle époque* department store had a huge, stained-glass-capped rotunda at its center. Generations of San Franciscans had come here to admire the finest Christmas tree in the city each year. When a luxury department store bought the corner and the closed department store and announced plans to demolish the landmark to build a new store, a cry of resistance burst out. To placate public dismay the owners announced that the stained-glass dome would be saved and incorporated into the new building. That was not enough—preservationists insisted that the whole building could be saved and demonstrated how, if the retailer wished, a new store could be fitted into the venerable structure. The owners then dropped their original architect and turned to the nationally lionized firm of Johnson, Burgee to redesign the proposed new building. Their redesign recycled not just the stained-glass dome but the four-story rotunda as well. The old dome and rotunda were given archeological treatment; the parts were numbered, cut apart, carefully disassembled, and then reassembled within the new building that was approved and constructed after a long and bitter battle.

This downtown trend of "partial preservation" has become a way for developers to "mitigate" the impact of their projects. At least a half-dozen partial or façade preservation projects have been completed in San Francisco's Financial District, and more are proposed. In private, architects dislike the idea; they prefer clean slates. Developers dislike it because it is always expensive. Preservationists dislike it because it is not real preservation. Planning commissions, caught in the middle and extremely reluctant to turn down any new investment in their downtowns, accept partial preservation proposals because they seem a compromise between the pressures for new development and the community's desire for at least a symbolic link with the vanishing urban past.

In-Town Victorian Neighborhoods

Adjacent to the core of most of the West's great cities are architecturally rich nineteenth-century residential areas that began declining when the automobile replaced the streetcar in this century. Con-

The rarest preservation is continuous preservation—the creation and uninterrupted care of fine buildings. Bullock's Wilshire department store of 1929, an Art Deco masterpiece in Los Angeles, symbolizes such continuous attention.

verted into rooming-house districts around the time of the Depression, these faded neighborhoods often contained the lion's share of a region's finest Victorian homes. Some, like Los Angeles' Bunker Hill, were cleared away by urban renewal, others by the natural workings of the real estate market as commercial uses spread into what were once residential areas. In the last twenty years, many of these well-designed, in-town districts have been reclaimed from decay and restored; their new residents were the first to become preservation-minded and to demand historic district protection.

The Mature Suburbs

Preservation is virtually automatic in the suburban ring built between the 1920s and the early 1960s. Zoning ordinances there both reflect and protect their usually homogeneous, middle-class populations; they preserve with such thoroughness that no one takes notice. Even landscaping patterns and maintenance standards are systematically enforced in politically independent suburban communities. The quiet "preservation issue" in these towns is whether or not to permit the legal subdivision of big houses into more than one living unit. To protect the homogeneity of suburban communities, such subdivision is almost never permitted, although in actuality living patterns are harder to regulate. While the attack on overregulation is momentarily ascendant in American political discourse, only under court orders have some American suburbs begun to alter, never mind abolish, their own often highly restrictive zoning and environmental standards. The changes in established suburbs have dealt more with the size of future building lots and permitted housing density than with existing housing.

Medium-Sized Cities

Medium-sized cities have seen the least preservation of all. Cities of this rank are generally eager to be rebuilding and modernizing. Even if the locality has stopped growing, the view is always to future growth. In nearly all medium-sized cities the highway strip leading out of town is the focus of virtually all economic activity and new development. Shopping centers on or beyond the strip attract most of the local shoppers, condemning the old downtown and its vintage buildings to obsolescence.

This is not exclusively a Western phenomenon, of course. Countless American cities have condemned their old downtowns by permitting—even encouraging—unlimited expansion at their fringes. In big cities and state capitals this desertion of the center has been masked by the explosive growth of governmental and financial bureaucracies that filled the void. But medium-sized cities have had no such expanding institutions to keep the old downtown alive. In some, even the fire, police, and administrative offices have moved out to the highway, removing the last major institutions from the city center.

Historically, the federal government set the standards in both quality design and land conservation in the Western states. Here the Point Wilson Lighthouse at the entrance to Puget Sound, built by the Coast Guard in 1914, epitomizes the federal government's Western installations.

Later-developed cities have been slow to adopt preservation. Many of them, such as Phoenix and San Jose, have swept away their past with a thoroughness that is both impressive and alarming. Americans have generally striven to have the newest of everything, perhaps Westerners more than most. In California, Bakersfield, San Jose, San Diego, and even Los Angeles have created small artificial ghettos outside of town to which historic buildings have been removed, cemeteries for history and architecture seen only by schoolchildren on field trips and devoid of natural economic life.

Small Towns

If architectural and historic preservation is now at least an element in the contemporary planning of major cities, the same is not true of small cities and towns. Of the many such places in the West, surprisingly few old ones remain unaltered. Here and there a few towns have become aware of their fragility and have protected themselves from harmful change through the mechanism of official historic districts. Jacksonville, Oregon, stands out in this regard. But what is most surprising is how very few they are. A single New England state probably has as many carefully preserved small towns as the entire West. The National Trust's Main Street program has been working to encourage the preservation of the best of the West's surviving nineteenth-century Main Streets. Today there are fourteen towns in Oregon, five in Washington, and one in California working to preserve their (usually red-brick) Main Streets with assistance from the National Trust.

Rural Areas: Ranching, Agriculture, and Mining

Generalizing about the state of architectural preservation in the West's rural areas—agricultural,

This scientifically accurate replica of a Navajo hogan at the Navajo National Monument in Arizona was built by the National Park Service to preserve the heritage of the Southwest.

ranching, and mining—is difficult both because of the vastness of the region and because of the great variety of its subregions. Most "spreads" in the West are far off the highway, invisible to the explorer. Western ranchers and farmers, famous for their love of privacy, rarely welcome uninvited visitors. No western state, it appears, has made a thorough survey of its ranching and farming heritage. The consolidation of small holdings into larger ones has left the Western landscape littered with abandoned ranch houses. When ranches and farms are consolidated, it is often the oldest houses that are made redundant. The passing of the great barns of Washington shows the dramatic effect that changes in farming technology are working in the West.

Many county historical societies have established outdoor museums to which representative ranch buildings and old farming machinery are removed. But these compounds, while important, are not *in situ* preservation and are no substitute for it.

Interestingly, it is the West's famous mining heritage that has seen the most dramatic preservation efforts. Places like California's great Empire Mine outside Grass Valley, in the Gold Country, or the ghost town of Bodie, near the Nevada border, or Idaho's Silver City, to name only three of the best sites, have seen exemplary preservation. This is curious since mining has been the most "rip and run" of the West's economic activities. But mining has a romantic mystique to which Westerners, and other Americans, are drawn.

Protected by the National Park Service, the cliff-house ruins at Keet Seel, built by the Anasazi almost a thousand years ago, are important links with mankind's collective past.

Organized Preservation in the West

The regional identity of the American West is principally focused on its stupendous natural wonders, from the Grand Canyon to the Pacific coast, rather than on its built environment. What man has built seems puny in comparison with the West's dramatic vistas: its mountains, forests, waters, and deserts. Preservation in the West began with natural preservation in California and the protection of the Yosemite Valley in the High Sierra. Other than reserving for public ownership certain ancient pueblo ruins in the Southwest, the federal government did little to preserve the heritage of the West.

Early Steps

In 1916 the National Park Service Organic Act, authored by San Francisco Bay Area congressman William Kent, was passed by Congress and signed by President Woodrow Wilson. The National Park Service's first director, Stephen T. Mather, began the important work of organizing and expanding the national parks. While the parks were created in order to preserve prime examples of both natural and man-made resources, at first the only man-made resources considered for national-park status were the Southwest's archeological treasures.

Not until the 1930s did historic preservation in a wider sense emerge as an important federal concern. President Franklin Roosevelt, a naval-history buff, included among his other federal employment programs during the depths of the Great Depression a survey of the nation's historic buildings. In 1933, the Historic American Buildings Survey (HABS) was set up within the National Park Service and funded by the New Deal's Civilian Works Administration, initially for only six months. Unemployed architects, historians, photographers, and draftsmen gathered information on outstanding buildings across the country. By World War II, when the project was suspended, more than six thousand structures had been documented and the information deposited in the Library of Congress. Most important, the HABS survey did not limit itself to public buildings and recorded choice buildings regardless of ownership.

The National Trust for Historic Preservation

In 1949 Congress chartered the National Trust for Historic Preservation in the United States, a private, nonprofit educational organization formed to encourage the preservation of significant historic buildings and sites and to foster public participation in the preservation of buildings, sites, objects, and ships important in American history and culture. About a third of the Trust's budget comes from a grant from the Department of the Interior's National Park Service. Membership dues (the Trust had 160,000 individual and organizational members in 1984), corporate and foundation gifts, endowment income, and merchandise sales make up the rest. In fiscal 1984 the federal grant to the National Trust amounted to $4.5 million.

The 1933 Spanish Renaissance post office in Yuma, Arizona, the best building in town, shows the high standards traditional in federal building a generation ago.

The National Trust is headquartered in Washington, D.C., and since the 1970s has established one field office and six regional offices, including one in San Francisco to cover the West. The Trust owns sixteen historic house museums, half of which are operated by local preservation organizations. The Trust has easements (legal covenants to protect façades and open spaces) on some seventy-five other historic properties across the nation. In the West, the National Trust has three historic properties, all in California: the Casa Amesti and Cooper-Molera Adobe, both in Monterey, and Filoli, an estate with fine gardens in San Mateo County.

While the Trust began as a custodian of great historic houses, it has evolved into more of a provider of technical assistance, advice, and support to state and local preservation groups across the country. It is increasingly a source of legal and tax information for private restoration and preservation efforts. The

Trust also provides grants and loans to aid preservation projects and conducts a varied information and educational program to increase knowledge of, and broaden support for, preservation across the country.

The Historic Preservation Act of 1966

A greater concern for the environment, including our historical architectural environment, emerged in the United States during the turbulent 1960s. Among its major legislative monuments was the National Historic Preservation Act of 1966, which, among other things, created the National Register of Historic Places to recognize properties of local, state, and national significance. Eligible for listing in the National Register are buildings, districts, sites, structures, and objects significant in American history, architecture, archeology, engineering, and culture. Nominations to the National Register can be made

Many different federal agencies hold public land in the West. The Bureau of Land Management protects the grazing lands that surround Silver City, Idaho, thus preserving the historic town's unspoiled setting. Federal land-use policies are of great importance in the West.

by an owner, a private citizen, or a preservation organization. Nominations are reviewed by a state review board composed of professionals in the fields of architecture, archeology, and history, and then approved (or not) by the state historic preservation officer. If approved, the nomination is forwarded to Washington where the Keeper of the National Register of Historic Places either accepts or rejects it. If accepted, the property is listed in the National Register.

The National Historic Preservation Act of 1966 also created the Advisory Council on Historic Preservation to review federally funded projects, such as highways, which might adversely affect properties listed in the National Register. This act also made preservation truly national by granting federal funds to set up state offices of historic preservation to survey each individual state, develop statewide preservation plans, nominate properties to the National Register, and help review federal projects that might affect historic properties. The state historic preservation officer, appointed by the governor, serves as the link between state and federal preservation efforts.

Preservation and Taxation: The Tax Reform Act of 1976

Historic preservation was given another important boost by the Tax Reform Act of 1976 (with its amendments of 1978), whereby Congress granted tax incentives to private owners of income-producing properties who restored their certified historic buildings (either local landmarks or National Register properties) according to architectural standards set by the secretary of the interior. These federal tax benefits were expanded in 1981 by a new investment tax credit allowing a 25 percent credit for rehabilitation of certified historic structures used for commercial purposes, as well as 20 and 15 percent credits for buildings over forty and thirty years old respectively. These favorable tax provisions were designed to draw capital into historic buildings needing restoration. Between 1976 and 1985 almost $7 billion was invested in historic buildings using these tax incentives. Among a variety of other projects, this infusion of capital produced over 54,000 rehabilitated housing units. Over half of this activity was in the Mid-Atlantic region with only some 5 percent in the West.

Finally, the Act authorized the creation of the Historic Preservation Fund which reserved a percentage of the federal royalties from off-shore oil tracts for distribution to the fifty states and territories for use in park and preservation projects. While this program is no longer available, many preservation projects were funded this way during the 1970s. In fact, there had not been so many federally financed preservation projects since the New Deal's Works Progress Administration of the 1930s.

Local Landmark Laws and Commissions

Preservation, of course, has never been limited to federal programs; local and state efforts have been important as well. The best measure of the increas-

The Timberline Lodge's new C. S. Price Wing, respectfully tucked behind the old lodge, shows how historic structures grow and adapt to new needs without losing their original character. This is preservation at its most sensitive.

ing national awareness of the importance of historic preservation has been the growth in the number of local (usually city) landmark and historic-district commissions. In 1955 there were only twenty in the entire country. By 1966 there were a hundred, and by 1976 there were nearly five hundred. Today their number has jumped to some one thousand. Many of these commissions watch over more than one historic district.

Local preservation commissions accept buildings as city landmarks and administer local historic-preservation ordinances. As a rule, these local ordinances permit landmark commissions to delay the demolition of an endangered certified landmark for up to a year, in order to try to find an alternative to tearing the building down. Some landmarks ordinances also protect publicly accessible interiors, but most apply only to the exteriors of landmark buildings. Unlike strong landmark controls against demolition in older Eastern cities such as Savannah, Charleston, Annapolis, New York, and Boston, Western cities have been less active in passing local landmark ordinances. Along with legal authority to delay demolition, public suasion is a landmark commission's best preservation tool.

Preservation Becomes a Part of City Planning

Increasingly in the West and all across the country, historic preservation is now seen by local planning commissions and departments as an essential ele-

Built by the Civilian Conservation Corps in 1935–1938 on Mount Hood, Oregon, the Timberline Lodge is now a historic piece of Western American architecture. A privately organized support group, The Friends of the Timberline Lodge, working with the management of Mount Hood National Park, has funded the meticulous and accurate restoration of the massive lodge with its handcrafted interiors and furnishings.

ment in comprehensive community planning. Even a few urban renewal agencies whose automatic response to old neighborhoods was to clear them away have become leaders in preservation. After the massive destruction wreaked by urban renewal in the 1960s, some city planners—after vigorous community protests—became aware that historic fabrics are irreplaceable, and that what often gets built in the place of historic buildings is socially and aesthetically inferior to what was there before. Planners came late to this realization; ordinary citizens were almost always more aware of the importance of urban conservation before the professionals. Many Western cities are only now digesting the dusty deserts that "urban renewal" created in their hearts. A classic example is Los Angeles, where, after clearing away the whole of the architecturally rich Victorian Bunker Hill neighborhood contiguous to the downtown in the 1960s, the Community Redevelopment Agency has today become the foremost local governmental agency urging and implementing the architectural preservation of the remaining historic downtown areas such as Broadway with its old movie palaces, and Spring Street, the old financial district, with its Beaux Arts and Art Deco office buildings.

"Zeroing Out" Historic Preservation

After the marked advances in federal leadership in historic preservation in the 1960s and 1970s, a fundamental shift occurred in the early 1980s under President Ronald Reagan. The new administration proposed "zeroing out" historic preservation in its first budget proposal. While supporting a program of tax incentives to encourage historic preservation, the Reagan administration still proposed to eliminate funding for the state historic preservation offices that must approve projects for the federal incentives. The Reagan administration threatened to leave no one to process the papers necessary for the tax credits. Here indeed was Catch-22. The Congress, responding to the urgings of preservationists and city leaders, who saw how effective the program was, refused to enact the Reagan program in full but did agree to cut federal funding for historic preservation from $42.5 million in 1981 to $26.5 million in 1982.

An even more ominous change, which Congress had passed in 1980, during the Carter administration, was an amendment to the National Historic Preservation Act requiring an owner's consent before listing a building on the National Register of Historic Places. Thus, today, official designation of the nation's heritage depends as much on who owns a particular building as on its architectural and historic merit.

The worst is perhaps yet to come. The Reagan administration is proposing that the Economic Recovery Tax Act of 1981, which granted tax credits for the rehabilitation of certified historic structures and has been such a marked success, be eliminated. Should this happen, one of the most beneficial structural incentives to preserve historic buildings will be destroyed.

PRESERVING THE WEST

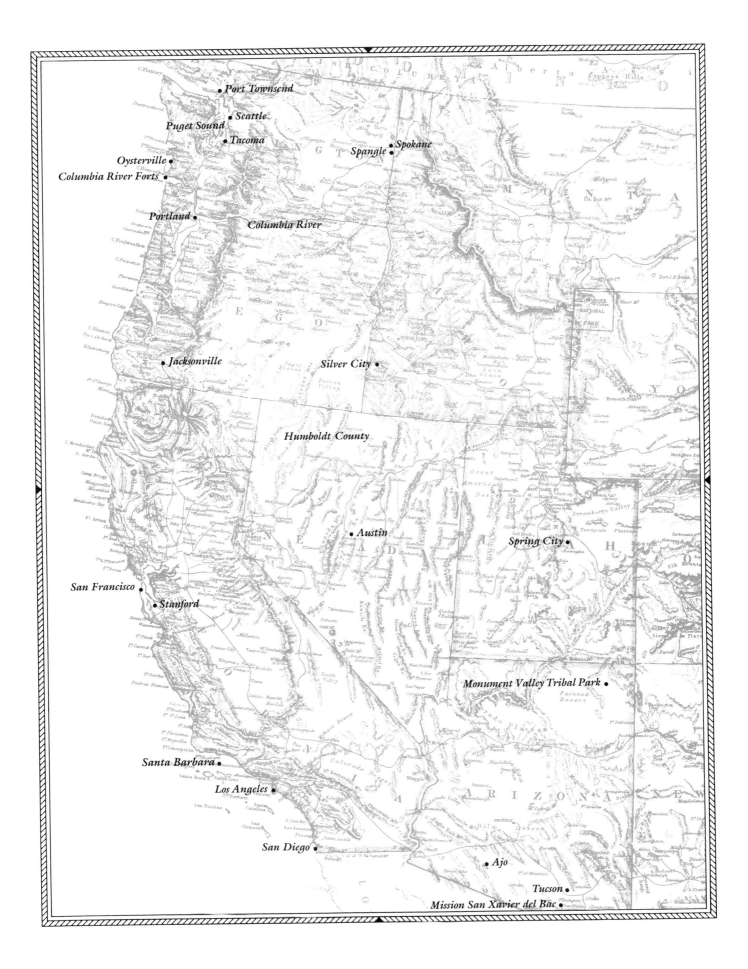

Port Townsend

Seattle

Puget Sound

Tacoma

Oysterville

Columbia River Forts

Portland

Columbia River

Spangle Spokane

Jacksonville

Silver City

Humboldt County

Austin

Spring City

San Francisco

Stanford

Monument Valley Tribal Park

Santa Barbara

Los Angeles

San Diego

Ajo

Tucson

Mission San Xavier del Bac

The carefully preserved ruins of a forked-stick hogan stand gaunt and weathered in the Monument Valley Tribal Park deep within the vast Navajo reservation. The Navajo Recreation and Resources Department guards these fragile ruins in their awesome red-sandstone setting.

PRESERVING TRADITIONAL FORMS:
THE NAVAJO HOGAN

Monument Valley Navajo Tribal Park, Arizona

ON THE poverty-stricken Indian reservations of the West, architectural preservation comes low on the list of community concerns. Pervasive unemployment, disease, and alcoholism make the struggle just to get by almost more than most people can handle. Many Native American communities are only all too happy to leave their old dwellings behind and to move into modern mobile homes or prefabricated housing. As a result, all over the West the Native American architectural heritage is fading fast.

One major exception to this sad story is found on the vast, twenty-five-thousand-square-mile Navajo reservation in the northeastern corner of Arizona. Rich oil, gas, and coal fields there provide royalties to the Navajo Tribal Council, which invests this money in community improvements. Among the most extraordinary preservation achievements in the American West is the 29,817-acre Monument Valley Tribal Park, located on the northern edge of this huge reservation. Established in 1958, this well-designed park has saved the unique red-sandstone landscape for both Navajos and visitors. Park police diligently patrol the valley to enforce respect for the land, its plants, and its artifacts. Some Navajo families remain here, following their flocks and living in traditional hogans. A two-lane road circles through the park, permitting visitors to experience this monumental landscape. Even the best-managed national parks have reason to envy the valley's serenity and immaculate condition.

Always more adaptable than other Native American communities, the Navajos have assimilated many modern elements into their tribal culture. Among them are mobile homes and contemporary houses, along with the ubiquitous and useful pickup truck. But unlike other tribes, which have turned their backs on their traditional architecture, the Navajos have preserved elements of their architectural past. Old hogans are often seen standing side by side with modern houses, a striking contrast. The traditional hogan is still the only place where certain curing ceremonies can be properly conducted. Then, too, some older people still prefer living in hogans. Other hogans are used for storage or as sheep sheds.

*Traditionally, Navajo dwellings were not gathered
in villages but scattered in widely dispersed
family camps. Modern resettlement plans have
gathered some of the Navajos in settlements,
leaving earlier houses such as these two
Anglo-style, red-sandstone dwellings behind.*

Another kind of preservation—the preservation of the traditional many-sided hogan *form*—can be seen in some new buildings, ranging from small stores to the tribal council's meeting place in Window Rock, Arizona, the tribe's capital, and the Navajo Community College. Navajo preservation embraces buildings, building forms, and entire landscapes—a remarkable achievement.

*Traditional polygonal hogans such as this one
silhouetted against a similarly shaped mesa are
preserved by the Navajo, who believe that certain
curing ceremonies can be conducted only within
them, not in modern rectangular houses.*

Begun about 1783 and consecrated in 1797, San Xavier del Bac church on the San Xavier Indian Reservation near Tucson is the greatest work of Spanish colonial architecture in the United States. Its dazzling white walls are periodically coated with white lime. Vermilion watercourses lead from the parapet to the ground.

RELIGION AND PRESERVATION

Mission San Xavier del Bac, Arizona

Flanking the great twin-towered church is the small mortuary chapel to the left and the long, one-story priests' residence to the right. The carved soft red-brick central façade contrasts with the bright white complex and foreshadows the polychromed retable behind the main altar inside. In front of the mission is a large plaza, the scene of fiestas and celebrations, that also serves as a parking lot.

ONE OF THE most spectacular preservation stories in the American West is that of the magnificent mission church of San Xavier del Bac on the Papago reservation some ten miles south of Tucson. Rising white and brilliant from the dusty green mesquite- and sage-covered desert, the twin towers and great dome of this two-hundred-year-old church are monuments to the enduring fusion of Papago piety and Spanish Catholicism. No mere "historical monument," though it certainly is that as well, Mission San Xavier is the spiritual center of the Indian, Mexican, and other Catholic peoples of southern Arizona and northern Sonora. Many come on pilgrimage to pray at the shrine of the Apostle to the Indies and to touch the head of the reclining figure of St. Francis Xavier in the great church's west chapel. Seemingly so serene in its open setting, which has changed little, the mission church of San Xavier has nevertheless had a

A wrought-iron rattlesnake, probably a twentieth-century embellishment, serves as the door handle to the great baroque church of San Xavier del Bac.

Massive volutes buttress the mission's lofty towers. One tower is capped by a cupola, the other is a roofless octagonal drum.

Bac means "place where the water emerges" and animals and men have been gathering here for water for thousands of years. A lion's head attached to a gate post looks out into the atrium, the mission's sand and cactus garden.

tumultuous history. But it has endured and stands today as the greatest example of Spanish colonial architecture and art north of the Mexican border.

Since time immemorial the native peoples gathered at Bac, an oasis in what became known as the Santa Cruz Valley. In 1692 Father Eusebio Kino, a Jesuit priest from the Tyrol, came to this favored spot to preach Christianity to the Pima Indians. In 1700 he laid the foundations here for a church that was never built. By 1732 there was a resident priest at Bac, but the Pima revolt of 1750 destroyed this remote mission. Four years later the mission was reestablished, but in 1767 the Jesuits were expelled from

Until recently, two smiling, crouching lions of carved wood flanked the sanctuary. The lion shown here, decorated for Easter, had human hands.

All around the interior of San Xavier is a heavy baroque cornice with a reddish Papago diamondback-rattlesnake design painted over it. Underneath the cornice is a knotted Franciscan cord in yellow with the stylized hem of a robe beneath it in burnt orange. These details symbolize the fusion of Papago and Christian culture.

the Spanish empire. In 1768 their place was taken by Franciscan priests from the college of Santa Cruz de Queretaro in Mexico City. The very next year the mission was sacked by the Apaches. Finally, in 1783, Father Juan Bautista Velderrain began the great church we see today. Built of fired brick coated with white lime plaster, it was completed and consecrated in 1797. The purpose of this great monument, facing south toward Mexico, was articulated in a Spanish report of 1804: "The reason for this ornate church at this last outpost of the frontier is not only to congregate Christian Pimas of the San Xavier village, but also to attract by its sheer beauty the unconverted Papagos and Gila Pimas beyond the frontier." Today

The richly colored retable behind the main altar is made
of fired brick, plastered, and then painted and gilded.
Its focal point is a statue of St. Francis Xavier dressed
in satin and velvet. Angels, saints, fantastic columns,
and carved draperies produce a sumptuous effect.

this impressive edifice still amazes—one can only imagine how it must have awed the native peoples at the turn of the nineteenth century.

In 1831 the newly independent Mexican state secularized all the missions and the priests left. There was to be no priest in residence at Bac until 1873; meanwhile the vast edifice slowly deteriorated. But the Christian Papagos loved their great church and did not destroy it. Finally, priests returned to take up residence once again. In 1906 Bishop Henri Granjon of Tucson restored the dilapidated church and expanded its outbuildings. Other extensive restorations were undertaken in 1942, and from 1968 to 1971.

As a functioning church, San Xavier is ineligible to receive federal or state funds, and the upkeep of this precious monument remains the responsibility of the reservation congregation and their friends. While the brick exterior is periodically coated with fresh white lime, the polychromed interior is not retouched except for the painted wainscoting along the base of the interior walls. Such careful restraint is rare in historic properties, especially churches, which all too often are overrestored. Subtle improvements are continually being made to the complex, but only if they do not disturb the original design. Over time the walls around the front garden have been rebuilt, and in 1968 the Mary Pew Benson Garden was added in the patio between the church and the priests' wing. San Xavier adapts to the needs of its congregation and links religion with preservation.

A woven-stick corral on the Papago reservation preserves an old form on the land. Saguaro cacti march in silent ranks up the hillside.

San Xavier continues to evolve. The cloistered inner patio alongside the church has been a corral, a cactus garden, and the site of a windmill. The fountain and new garden, still immature, were added between 1968 and 1971. Continuing the theme of animal-inspired decorations, small ceramic doves are visible atop the parapet and fountain.

Bishop Henri Granjon erected these mission-style
arcades behind the church and patio in 1906, to mask garages and
other service buildings added when the mission
was restored and expanded. Mission San Xavier has changed
while still preserving its architectural unity.

Three traditional adobe bricks lie atop a walkway of smaller, red-clay American bricks. Long neglected, the Southwest's adobe heritage is as fragile as the sunbaked earthen bricks it is made of.

Historic Tucson's architecture is a fusion of Sonoran (or Mexican) and Anglo, (or American) elements. Lightweight, gabled roofs built with milled lumber succeeded the original flat mud roofs when Arizona became part of the United States, producing Transformed Sonoran buildings such as this row on N. Meyer Street in the El Presidio Historic District.

TWO BROWN BARRIOS

Tucson, Arizona

Retrenchment by the overextended Spanish empire led to the reorganization of Mexico's frontier fortifications in the 1770s under Charles III's royal regulations for presidios. Tucson was established in the Santa Cruz Valley in August 1775 as part of this consolidated presidial cordon. Christened San Augustín del Tucson by Hugh O'Connor, the Spanish imperial commander of New Spain's Mexican frontier, the remote settlement grew in a haphazard way around the fort. Adobe technology was imported from Spanish Mexico and rude buildings sprang up utilizing this low-cost material. Only about a thousand Christian Indians and mestizos lived in the area by the 1840s.

Tucson became part of the United States through

The side door and courtlike backyard of a simple adobe house in the El Presidio Historic District in Tucson show the typical state of adobes in the Southwest's surviving old neighborhoods.

the Gadsden Purchase of 1853. But the adobe town
was not attractive to the Anglos who migrated there.
In 1858 one unhappy visitor lamented that "not a
white wall nor a green tree was to be seen there."
The local adobe buildings were transformed by the
Anglos, with waterproof wooden roofs replacing flat
mud ones and wooden floors covering earthen ones.
In this way the Transformed Sonoran building style
was born; it has continued fitfully to the present.

As soon as they could, the American settlers built
modern buildings of hard, fired red brick. Using
styles from back East, they created the territorial
style, which was prevalent in Anglo buildings until
the early years of the twentieth century. The new-
comers also laid out an orderly grid of new streets
around the casually evolved Mexican-era core. When
the Southern Pacific Railroad arrived in 1880, the
city quickly took on the characteristic North American form of a substantial brick downtown, which displaced the earlier adobe buildings. Between the new
Anglo downtown and the new Anglo residential districts, a band of old adobes survived, mainly housing
the poorer Mexican-Americans. Poverty preserved
the old buildings in the unfashionable parts of town.

While the genuine adobe houses of old Tucson
were held in contempt, a taste for mission and Moorish decoration emerged among the wealthy during
the first decade of the twentieth century. Local architects such as Henry Trost blended these motifs
with influences from as far away as Chicago and Los
Angeles. This fashion was the first sign of the emer-

Adobe buildings are exceedingly fragile; if not continually plastered and repaired, they melt in the rain. This ruined Sonoran adobe on N. Meyer Street in a National Register district has wasted away to a mere shell.

gence of a deliberately regional style in Tucson architecture.

Although the Tucson Historical Committee was organized in 1960, preservation got off to a slow start. Massive urban renewal scraped away most of the nineteenth-century downtown between 1965 and

(Top and middle): New buildings in the historic districts must conform to the area. Here a brand-new adobe is under construction at Convent and Kennedy streets in the Barrio Historico, using smaller, petroleum-stabilized modern adobe bricks set atop a cinder-block foundation.

(Bottom): Large expanses of glass and American-style hedges, are awkward intrusions along the ragged edges of Tucson's historic districts.

1970. New development in the expanding east side of the city siphoned off most of the retail shoppers, leaving behind a moribund downtown, which was rebuilt with high-rise banks, office buildings, and new hotels with no particular regional flavor. A couple of specimen adobes were restored and opened as museums in connection with a new downtown cultural center, but the city of Tucson did not publish a list of historical sites until 1969, after most of the old Anglo downtown had been cleared away. Visitors to Tucson are today more likely to visit Old Tucson, a movie set outside of town built in 1939, than the real city.

In the 1970s preservation became much more widely accepted in Tucson. Residents of the surviving adobe Mexican-American barrios were mobilized when a freeway threatened to demolish parts of their community. Some University of Arizona College of Architecture faculty began to study the local vernacular buildings that survived, and in 1972 a study entitled *Barrio Historico: Tucson* explained the evolution of adobe building in the city. At the same time, grassroots neighborhood organizations formed to encourage the restoration of the old barrios. It was often younger Anglo-and-brown mixed couples who best understood the unique cultural heritage of Tucson and who saw architectural preservation as more than the embalming of specimen adobes attached to museums. For them preservation meant protecting ra-

In the 1900s the Southwest saw a burst of
deliberately regional architecture in the various
revivals that became so popular: Pueblo revival,
mission revival, and Spanish colonial revival. This
mission revival adobe, with its arcade and emphatic
parapet, is a prime example of the type.

cially mixed neighborhoods where the diverse peoples of the Southwest, usually highly segregated,
could live together. In 1975 both adobe districts—El
Presidio and Barrio Historico—were listed on the National Register of Historic Places. Late-nineteenth-
century Anglo neighborhoods such as Armory Park
also became strongly preservationist, and 75 percent
of the property owners there petitioned the city for
designation as a historic district (the city requires the
agreement of at least 65 percent in order to grant
such designations). Today Tucson has five National
Register districts and four city-designated historic
districts, preserving both traditional adobes and
Anglo buildings built as late as the early 1930s.

Designs inspired by Chicago architect Louis Sullivan also
appeared in Tucson at the turn of the century. Bold forms
covered with intricate, geometric ornamentation
characterized these modern designs. After long neglect,
these rarities, especially the works of Henry Trost, are now
recognized as local treasures worthy of preservation.

The shaded arcades embracing Ajo's plaza are well adapted to the region's hot climate. This well-planned mission-style company town is preserved intact by Phelps Dodge.

COMPANY TOWN: PRESERVATION THROUGH SINGLE OWNERSHIP

Ajo, Arizona

Most of the settlements and buildings in the West were built by individuals filling in the checkerboard grid of uniform town plots. Buildings were constructed without regard to a conscious city plan; what coherence settlements achieved was due to the real estate market's idea of the relative value of individual sites—or the accidental fires that wiped out sections of towns, which were then rebuilt under the influence of the architectural style prevalent at the moment. Seattle's Pioneer Square of the late 1880s and San Francisco's retail district of the post-1906 era are big-city examples of such coherence by accident.

The only exceptions to this haphazard pattern of development were corporately owned and developed company towns built in mining or lumbering districts. Nevertheless, most of these towns were built with little regard for architectural embellishment. Of these planned communities, perhaps the best remaining one is the copper mining town of Ajo, Arizona. It was built about 1916 next to one of the world's earliest and largest open-pit mines. The New Cornelia Copper Company, backed by the Lewisohn financial interests of New York, adopted the mission style for the new town. The previous settlement, located directly over the ore body, was cleared away for the new open-pit mine. Next to the new mine a checkerboard grid was laid out, a plaza at its center, with the town's railroad station on one side and arcades on two others. Here were the company store, other shops, and a movie house. Directly across from the railroad station two churches were built, one

Catholic and one Protestant. Between the churches a street was laid out climbing a gentle slope. An imposing public school was situated at the head of this one-block-long street. The plaza itself was formally landscaped, with a fountain at its center and irrigated lawns and rows of palm trees, creating a shaded oasis in the harsh Sonoran desert. Beyond this formal core the modest houses of the mostly Mexican mine workers spread out over the grid of streets.

The New Cornelia Copper Company was eventu-

Mature palms and green lawns make Ajo's central plaza a welcome island in the Sonoran desert.

A wall pierced with arches masks the railroad tracks that skirt the plaza. Imported palms lend elegance to this desert mining community.

ally absorbed into the parent Calumet and Arizona Mining Company, which was bought in turn by New York–based Phelps Dodge in 1931. While the fortunes of the copper industry rose and fell, Ajo's pleasant core was carefully maintained and preserved by its distant owners. The Ajo Improvement Company, with offices next to the railroad station, has kept the plaza and its company store the focus of the settlement. No strip development along the highway leading out of town has been permitted to bleed the center dry. Now that the palms in the plaza have matured, the town presents a pleasing, settled appearance. But what copper gave, copper can take away. Depressed prices in world markets coupled with state and federal clean-air regulations, which require a reduction in sulfur dioxide and particulate emissions from the Ajo smelter, have raised serious

questions about the future of the mine, its eleven hundred workers, and the coherent town that serves them.

Perhaps Ajo's future preservation will echo that of another Phelps Dodge town, Tyrone, New Mexico. The influence of the wife of one of the principals of the company resulted in the commissioning of famed New York architect Bertram G. Goodhue to design a mission-style town there in 1916. But after World War I the copper industry went into a deep depression and by 1921 the mine at Tyrone was closed. From 1932 to 1940 the handsome town site functioned as the Rancho Los Piños Guest Ranch, until the increased demands of the war effort reactivated the mine in 1941. Ajo's future preservation may also depend on its conversion into a retirement or recreational community.

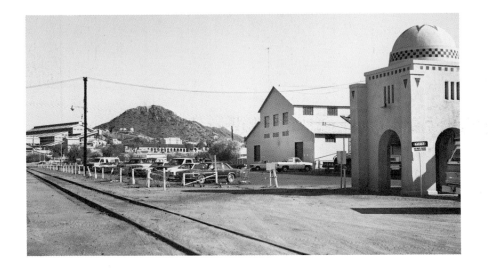

Beyond the Moorish-style dome that anchors one corner of Ajo's plaza is the straightforward industrial architecture of the copper mine and its giant smelter. (Right): A small front-yard shrine reflects the mission heritage of the Southwest. Such folk-art embellishments are rare but welcome gestures that lend texture to the regional landscape.

The ordinary housing stock of San Francisco is continually refurbished, often with great sensitivity to the character of the building. Here an 1890s apartment building on Waller Street in the Duboce Triangle area is being restored by its new owners.

One of the best things that ever happened in San Francisco was the FACE (Federally Assisted Code Enforcement) program of the late 1960s and early 1970s, whereby the city chose declining neighborhoods for building inspections and then offered owners low-interest federal loans to rehabilitate their buildings. Whole areas of the city were kept from declining while raising housing costs only incrementally instead of catastrophically. Beulah Street in the Haight-Ashbury was a FACE area.

STATE-OF-THE-ART PRESERVATION

San Francisco, California

A CITY OF great prosperity, San Francisco has felt the pressure to tear down low-rise buildings to build larger ones, both downtown and in the surrounding neighborhoods, more intensely than most large American cities. On Russian Hill, long famous for its spectacular views, a string of high-rises sprang up along Green Street in the 1960s, changing the character of the formerly low-rise neighborhood and threatening to flood it with cars and people. Long a city with an active planning commission and department, the city's first response to the sixties high-rise boom was to confine such structures to the heart of the downtown or the tops of the surrounding hills, where they would block the fewest views. But this proved not to be enough for San Franciscans, who, more than most city dwellers, were not ready to accept the degradation of their attractive urban environment as inevitable.

When an especially wall-like, view-blocking apartment building suddenly appeared on the low-rise waterfront in 1962, it appeared that the city might soon be cut off completely from views of the bay. A movement began among the many neighborhood organizations to reassess permitted building heights in residential areas. Because of organized neighborhood political pressure, a citywide residential rezoning program was launched by the City Planning Commission that down-zoned almost all the city's richly diverse neighborhoods to make permitted heights conform to existing patterns. This collective

Preservation and restoration are seen citywide in San Francisco. Here an ornate Victorian house built in the 1880s undergoes restoration on Masonic Avenue in the Haight-Ashbury. Since most of San Francisco's Victorian houses were built of rot-resistant redwood, many have survived to be restored.

Fillmore Street is typical of the many neighborhood commercial strips that developed along transit lines during the late nineteenth and early twentieth centuries. Today, preservation in San Francisco is increasingly concerned with conserving and enhancing these walkable shopping streets.

The survival, preservation, and restoration of commercial design is especially rare. Restaurants are occasional exceptions to this rule. The Art Deco Elite Cafe on Fillmore Street was recently restored, preserving its original façade, neon sign, booths, furniture, and fixtures while adding such features as the etched glass divider designed to harmonize with the vintage interior.

public change has resulted in the preservation of many vintage buildings and established neighborhoods, since it is uneconomical to demolish two- to four-story-high structures to build new ones of only slightly larger size. Another result of this down-zoning has been the continual filling-in of gaps in the urban fabric such as closed service stations, empty lots, and old parking garages. One by one, these sites are giving way to expensive, high-style condominiums, usually the same height as their largest neighbor.

No architectural or design controls mandate particular styles in San Francisco. The high costs of land and building, combined with the sophistication of the San Francisco market, generally result in quality design. The ugly (if inexpensive) stucco boxes of the 1960s are no longer being built. Every year, more restored Victorian and period buildings grace the city as asbestos shingle and other "improvements" of the 1940s and 1950s are pried off and façades are rebuilt out of redwood.

Some San Franciscans have moved beyond a concern for the preservation of buildings to the preservation of entire communities—of residents along

(Top and middle): In the early 1980s, San Francisco's famous cable-car system underwent a total rebuilding in order to preserve it. All tracks were replaced and the powerhouse and car barn at Washington and Mason streets was completely rebuilt within its old four walls. The brick powerhouse had been hastily thrown up after the earthquake and fire of 1906 and was quite fragile. Ten percent of the cost of this massive project was raised from private donations; 90 percent came from a federal grant to this National Register transportation system.

(Bottom): The new headquarters of Levi Strauss in a former warehouse district at the foot of Telegraph Hill is a combination of preserved and redesigned old buildings, such as the 1903 Italian Swiss Colony Warehouse here on the right, and terraced new buildings that step back from the red-brick district toward the hill. The new buildings were designed by HOK and the attractive park by Lawrence Halprin Associates.

with residences. In low-income areas such as Chinatown and in the high-density downtown Tenderloin district, new community organizations are seeking ways to preserve and improve low-cost housing without driving out the residents. This is exceedingly difficult to achieve in a free-market economy, where each piece of individually owned real estate irresistibly moves up to a more remunerative use. Some nonprofit community corporations have been formed in Chinatown to rehabilitate low-rise, low-income apartments and residential hotels without dramatic escalations in rent. In the Tenderloin, the city's largest reservoir of low-rent hotels and apartments, the North of Market Planning Coalition worked to make the developers of three new luxury tourist hotels in the neighborhood set aside $8.5 million to rehabilitate nearby residential hotel rooms. Tenderloin residents are attempting to prevent the conversion of residential hotels into tourist accommodations that can produce higher incomes. City permission must be secured to convert hotels from one use to another, and residents are organizing to make their interests heard at city hall. Not surprisingly, this is an uphill fight.

(Left and opposite): The Citicorp tower by William Perrira and Associates incorporates as its Sansome Street entrance the façade of the historic London-Paris-Anglo National Bank, which was designed by Albert Pissis in 1904 and expanded sympathetically by George Kelham in 1936. With a glass-roofed café in the white-marble-lined Beaux Arts bank, this has become an oasis in the new high-rise downtown.

Today, preserving San Francisco's well-known social diversity is a much more difficult task than preserving its architectural variety. The booming downtown is putting enormous pressure on rents and housing costs, as thousands of high-paying jobs in new high-rise office buildings create more demand for the city's limited housing stock. The City Planning Commission is attempting to establish a system whereby a small part of the wealth that is pouring into the downtown office boom is diverted to build or rehabilitate low-income units in other parts of the city. Office developers are being required to assist in producing low-income housing in return for permission to build. But seeing the city as a whole of interrelated parts is something new, and many developers resist it.

Meanwhile, partial or façade preservation has been the unsatisfactory compromise struck between the enormous pressure to build high-rises on every lot downtown and the undisputed architectural quality of the historic Financial and Retail districts. A flurry of occasionally good but often bad partial preservation projects are under construction. Preservationists in San Francisco contend that there are few if any good partial preservation compromises, and vigorously pursue the preservation of entire buildings, not parts of them.

That San Francisco's Financial and Retail districts are architecturally distinguished has been always obvious but only recently documented. In 1979 the membership-supported Foundation for San Francisco's Architectural Heritage published a state-of-the-art architectural survey of every building in the city's core, pinpointing the quality designs essential to the character of the rapidly changing downtown. The City Planning Commission has adopted that survey's list of prime buildings as elements of the city worth preserving. But the existing height allowances and zoning in the old core—established many years ago when an interest in the architectural heritage downtown was not perceived as a key factor in making the city attractive to business—threaten most of

Because of the importance of the block of which the old California-Pacific Building is a part, the City Planning Commission required that the developer preserve it and build a taller tower alongside. However, the interior of the old building was destroyed and floors were extended from the new building into the old, sometimes cutting right across the old building's windows.

these buildings by encouraging their replacement with taller structures, despite the fact that the buildings themselves have always been profitable and well maintained.

With the assistance of a grant from the National Trust, the Foundation for San Francisco's Architectural Heritage is working to devise a strategy for architectural preservation in the intensely pressured downtown. One of its goals is to find a way to sell the developable space over low-rise, high-quality historic buildings downtown and transfer it to other sites in the satellite South of Market area toward which the office core is expanding. The idea is to protect the values of the owners of the property on which the vintage buildings stand by permitting them to profit from *not* demolishing their buildings. This plan, called a transfer of development rights, will depend on the city's adopting strong demolition controls on historic buildings, down-zoning both downtown and the areas to which development rights can be transferred, and then setting up an "as of right" system, whereby a developer is certain that the development rights bought in the old core can be applied to a bigger building on a different site. In this way the city could preserve the best of its downtown without injuring the interests of private property owners. This is a premier example of the new trend of making preservation a part of comprehensive city planning.

The refurbishing of the 1910 Clayton Hotel on Clay Street in Chinatown was undertaken by the Chinese Community Housing Corporation to provide low-cost housing for the elderly. An unusual colored-tile border frames the upper stories of the Edwardian hotel. The building was made fresh and attractive without destroying its best old features, including the metal sign. Best of all, it is still a low-cost residential hotel.

Willis Polk's Hallidie Building of 1917, the world's first glass-curtain-walled building and the single most important work of architecture in San Francisco, has been restored as prime office space. Favorable tax treatment helped make this an attractive investment while preserving an architectural jewel.

*The red-tile-roofed, golden-yellow-sandstone Old
Quad at the heart of the Stanford campus was
designed by Shepley, Rutan and Coolidge in
collaboration with Frederick Law Olmsted in 1887.
Its arcades linked together all the buildings
into one interconnected "megastructure."*

EARTHQUAKES AND PRESERVATION: RECONSTRUCTION OF STANFORD'S OLD QUAD

PHOTOGRAPHS: RANDOLPH LANGENBACH

Stanford, California

Founded in 1885 and richly endowed with Leland Stanford's Central Pacific Railroad millions, Stanford University is justly proud of its distinguished Boston-designed campus. Located not far from the San Andreas fault, the university has faced what is perhaps the ultimate preservation problem in the seismic West: how to bring old and architecturally distinguished brick and stone buildings up to modern earthquake-resistance standards. Its solution was expensive, technologically challenging, and artistically successful.

Stanford is not unfamiliar with seismic events—in 1906, the famous San Francisco earthquake threw down Memorial Church, Memorial Arch, and other buildings on campus. Fortunately, the stone-clad Old Quad, the center of the Richardsonian/mission-style campus, with its extra-wide footings, was only partially damaged. It is these fine buildings, along with their arcades and courtyards, that are the heart of Stanford's architectural identity.

But surviving one earthquake is not a guarantee of surviving another. The trustees decided to strengthen the Old Quad while preserving its ar-

A bust of philanthropist Leland Stanford looks out from the recently reinforced History Corner. Behind its ornate but fragile masonry walls is a brand-new concrete-and-steel core built to withstand most earth tremors.

Building by building, the unreinforced masonry structures are being strengthened with a modern reinforced concrete shell erected behind, and attached to, the old stones.

chitectural beauty. The firm of Esherick Homsey Dodge and Davis, the architect-preservers of San Francisco's Cannery, led the partnership that preserved the key Old Quad buildings and designed stronger new buildings within their historic shells. In a phased program, sections of the historic quad were partially disassembled. Red-tile roofs were removed (and the old tiles stored), wood floors and wood-and-plaster interior partitions were scooped out, and new steel-bar-reinforced concrete structures were built within the old brick and sandstone-veneer walls. To secure the fine (but fragile) old stonework, reinforcing bars were sunk into holes drilled two feet apart

Once reerected, the arcades should be able to withstand future tremors better than unreinforced brick and stone.

in the backs of the old walls to weld them to the new concrete-and-steel core. Once the old walls had been strengthened from behind, new interiors were constructed. Interior spaces were rethought to eke out as much usable space as possible without altering the façades.

In one Old Quad building, which had been completed in 1899 as an auditorium and later subdivided

Stanford's reinforced arcades are natural places for people to meet. Preservation here furthers the coherence of a great university.

to house the business school, a three-story building with basement was turned into six usable floors by digging down for a subbasement and redesigning the old attic. A two-level TV studio was inserted into the basement, and room was designed upstairs for the sociology and communications departments.

At History Corner—a highly visible part of the Old Quad, and to a Stanford student a memorable one, because of its classrooms—the new program was less intensive. The architects rebuilt the two original stories, using harder oak to duplicate the old doors and wainscoting, and new cast- and wrought-iron segments to augment the old stairs. They also converted the attic to a usable classroom floor, with "roof slots" creating terraces looking out over the inner court, but with no change to the roof visible from the Palm Drive front. Reanchored in a corner niche under the inscription *History,* Leland Stanford's stone bust still surveys a remarkable philanthropic and architectural achievement. The university has finished restoring one batch of buildings; in the future, this meticulous work will be extended to other parts of the campus.

The rebuilt interior of the History Corner building preserved and reused the 1880s iron balustrades within the new reinforced-concrete building.

The back, or inside, of History Corner shows the "roof slots," or roof terraces, introduced into the attic stories to get a third usable floor out of a two-story building.

Santa Barbara has taken to heart the motto carved in Spanish over the ceremonial entrance to architect William Mooser's courthouse. "God gave us the country. The skill of man hath built the town."

DESIGN CONTROL
AND THE PRESERVATION
OF URBAN FORM

Santa Barbara, California

SANTA Barbara is a unique city socially and architecturally, and in its concept of preservation. A Spanish colonial fort, mission, and seaport established in the 1780s, it has a gentle climate and beautiful situation that drew wealthy, cultured Midwesterners and Easterners to it after the completion of the railroad in 1887. Along with Monterey, it had been one of the most important settlements during the colonial and Mexican periods, and its relatively elaborate mission of the late eighteenth century had never been abandoned. These new people settled in postrailroad Santa Barbara because of its charm and soon set out to preserve and enhance it. The private but influential Community Arts Association encouraged the restoration of adobes, as well as beautification of the city through public landscaping and use of a deliberately regional Spanish style. This association also set up a Community Drafting Room, which helped commercial and residential builders design in the white-walled, red-tile-roofed style. In the Paseo de la Guerra project of 1922, a group of old adobes was restored and made the centerpiece of a congenial pedestrian-oriented development of shops and restaurants in the revived Spanish style.

When the severe earthquake of 1925 destroyed many of the buildings along Santa Barbara's typical brick Victorian and Edwardian main street, the city council empowered a new Architectural Board of Review to pass on every building permit issued. This board attempted to require every building owner to reconstruct in the Spanish style, although legal challenges succeeded in striking this down a year later as an infringement on private property rights. But many investors wanted to build in the new "historic" style, and the city that emerged from the post-earthquake reconstruction and expansion had a new coherence and a distinctive look.

Santa Barbara, the patron saint of soldiers, has a tower as her emblem. Here that symbol appears carved in soft Refugio Canyon sandstone on the landmark Santa Barbara County Court House of 1929.

*The courthouse's assembly room boasts a vivid,
panoramic mural by Dan Sayre Groesbeck depicting
the history of Santa Barbara. The room and its
furnishings are a perfectly preserved monument
of 1920s Spanish style.*

The city was fortunate to rebuild when it did, for the 1920s were a golden age for architecture in California. Designed by the San Francisco architect William Mooser in 1929, the new courthouse that rose in the heart of the city is "historic" in its feel and a brilliant modern design at the same time. While Mission Santa Barbara (1812–1820) was the city's great monument from the colonial period, the Courthouse is its American architectural symbol and achievement. Church and state, in a classic pattern, have set the design standards for the rest of the city. This influence has filtered down to simple houses, schools, churches, gas stations, and, later, motels.

Today Santa Barbara has a strong landmark ordinance to protect its old buildings, a height-control ordinance that encourages the preservation of old, low-rise buildings, and a 1967 city charter that mandates Spanish or Santa Barbara style architecture. This civic policy is overseen by a landmarks committee and the Architectural Board of Review that pass on every building proposal within designated architecturally sensitive districts.

Although ten years ago most architects resisted working within the look mandated by the city, today investors and designers realize that Santa Barbara is unique, that it has made itself so, and that it is as much of a design challenge to work within one style as it is to design something determinedly "new." After sixty years of propaganda and building, Santa

Now more than fifty years old, the Santa Barbara County Court House will need increasing care. Here sculptor Ettore Cadorin's carved sandstone fountain, The Spirit of the Ocean, undergoes restoration.

Robust and emphatic, this new wall with its fountain, designed by Santa Barbara architect Henry Lenny, artistically masks a parking lot and continues the streetscape in downtown Santa Barbara.

Barbara does have a special urban, landscape, and design heritage that is now generally recognized and prized. Then, too, California Polytechnic in nearby San Luis Obispo has graduated several locally active architects who *want* to design imaginatively within the recognized local tradition they prize. A renaissance of good contemporary design, almost on a par with the creative 1920s, is now under way.

The formulas of design-control ordinances are useful even in buildings that are not good designs. This office building on E. Carrillo Street would be only more disruptive if not surfaced in stucco and roofed with red tiles.

Good new designs done within design-control ordinances, such as this brand-new arcaded office building at 222 E. Carrillo Street by the firm of Edwards and Pitman, can be large and yet add to Santa Barbara's character.

James Oviatt commissioned the firm of Walker and Eisen to design Los Angeles' most prestigious men's clothing store right before the Crash of 1929; his own penthouse was built atop it. The building has recently been restored; a swank restaurant now occupies the grand first-floor interior and offices the upper floors. (Top left): Custom-designed Lalique glass with an orange motif ornaments the elevator doors. (Right): The new metal lobby gates designed by Jean Clyde Mason harmonize perfectly.

THE HERITAGE
OF THE MODERN AGE

The Los Angeles Basin, California

IN SIZE and dynamism, the greatest city in the American West is Los Angeles. Its architectural treasures—mostly from the modern period—match its fame. But only recently has preservation emerged as an force to be reckoned with in this vital city.

Founded by the Spanish in 1781, Los Angeles did not emerge as an important city until the 1880s and the arrival of the railroad. The development of the oil industry in the 1920s made Los Angeles a wealthy city with a go-go mentality. The city's psychology was also deeply influenced by its most famous industry, moviemaking. The taste for fantasy, extravagance, and, its critics would contend, impermanence marks much of the region's early-twentieth-century design. The great modern Los Angeles architect Richard J. Neutra claimed that movie sets confused architectural tastes in L.A., producing half-timber English peasant cottages next to French provincial châteaux next to mission-bell adobes next to Arabian minarets next to Georgian mansions. Neutra wrote: "A Cape Cod fisherman's hut (far from beach and fish) appears side by side with a realtor's field office seemingly built by Hopi Indians"—all built of two-by-fours, chicken wire, and stucco. The city's famous "programmatic architecture"—ice-cream stands shaped like igloos or tamale stands shaped like tamales or classy restaurants shaped like derbies—is an extreme example of this taste for whimsy and instant identity.

But such a dismissive picture of Los Angeles' architectural heritage is misleading. For beside its flamboyant, pseudo-historical productions in lath and plaster have arisen first-class works of modern de-

The Wiltern-Pellisier Building on Wilshire Boulevard at Western was designed by Morgan, Walls and Clements in 1930 as a theater and office tower with sidewalk shops. When the turquoise-tile-clad Moderne skyscraper was threatened with demolition, the Los Angeles Conservancy rallied public opinion and it was made a city landmark. Favorable tax treatment has spurred its restoration by a private developer.

The publicly owned Pan-Pacific Auditorium in the Fairfax district sits in a park and continues to decay. A National Register property, it was designed in 1935 by Wurdeman and Becket and is the major monument of the Streamline Moderne style in Los Angeles. Efforts are afoot to adapt it to private retail and public cultural uses, but progress is slow.

sign. Innovative designers flourished here during the booming 1920s (and a decade earlier in nearby Pasadena) and continued to build through the 1930s, when the rest of the country was stagnating.

Through the 1940s and 1950s Southern California continued to build, and in many cases produced designs that stand at the apex of their era. By the 1950s, in fact, Southern California began to export its design

A colorfully tiled pyramid and a torch of knowledge cap Bertram Goodhue's last building, the Los Angeles Public Library of 1921–1926 in the heart of downtown Los Angeles. Among the most important architectural works in Southern California, it has nonetheless been under constant attack by city officials for "functional inadequacies." Lee Lawrie sculpted the figures on the façade. The Greek figure on the left represents the Thinker, the Egyptian figure on the right, the Writer. The motto inscribed on the open book translates as "A lamp to my feet, a light to my paths."

influence to the rest of the nation and the world. The Los Angeles basin now boasts some of the most important architectural works of the modern age. The challenge here lies in increasing the public's aware- ness of the high value of the early modern works that survive.

Such an awareness is slowly but surely taking hold in Southern California. After a typical phase of tear-

Santa Monica's Horatio West Court of 1919, designed by Irving Gill, is one of the finest modern designs in California and is still fresh today. It was built on a low budget on a typical house lot; its courtyard configuration was Southern California's regional answer to the multifamily dwelling. Its new architect-owner has restored it with great sensitivity while accommodating to the changes in the city. A simple and appropriate apple-green fence added recently looks like part of the original design and enhances the court's privacy and security while permitting passersby to appreciate the original building.

it-all-down urban renewal, the city of Los Angeles, while still avidly looking forward to new development, has begun to work toward the preservation of its cultural heritage. Broadway, the old streetcar-era main street, and Spring Street, the early-twentieth-century financial district, were both left behind as the focus of the downtown shifted west toward the new freeway. Broadway has now become the most important Mexican-American shopping district north of the border. Preservation problems loom there because of new earthquake codes and the fact that in many cases only the ground floor of multistory brick buildings is occupied. But the city is aware of the importance of the street and its great old movie palaces, which now show Spanish-language films, and the stretch between Third and Ninth streets has been made a National Register district. A block away is the Spring Street Historic District, with its Art Deco office blocks and old Beaux Arts banks that the Community Redevelopment Agency is helping to convert to new uses, including inner-city housing. The agency also has its own office in a vintage Spring Street building.

On the private front, an active citywide preservation group organized in 1978, the Los Angeles Con-

servancy, is imaginatively working to promote public consciousness of the architectural riches of the city. With locally keyed programs, such as its Cruisin' L.A. tour, which highlights the heritage of the automotive environment, and good coverage in the *Los Angeles Times,* the message is getting out that Los Angeles should be proud of its place in American design.

Other private efforts, such as the Friends of the Schindler House, are active as well. That group purchased the landmark Rudolph M. Schindler House and Studio in Hollywood in 1980 with the help of a $160,000 grant from the State of California's Office of Historic Preservation. More aid came from the National Endowment for the Arts in planning the restoration and adaptive reuse of the property as a gallery and museum. More money is needed to continue the project, but at least the landmark has been saved from demolition. In nearby Pasadena, Greene and Greene's masterpiece, the Gamble House of 1908, another national monument in residential design, has been preserved by the University of Southern California and the city of Pasadena working together. These are important beginnings, for they preserve two of the finest works of regional domestic architecture in the nation.

Inside the Schindler House the "improvements" of later periods are being carefully removed. White paint is being stripped from the originally natural redwood beams and raw cast-concrete walls. To the left is one of the few original wood-and-canvas Schindler-designed furnishings left in the low-budget house.

A detail of the redwood mullions conveys the ultramodern feeling of this historic house. Now undergoing restoration by the Friends of the Schindler House, it serves as a gallery and museum.

In the past few years, some private developers have become active in the restoration and reuse of fine Moderne office buildings such as the Wiltern-Pellisier Building on Wilshire Boulevard or the Oviatt Building near Pershing Square downtown. Some vintage and Art Deco movie theaters have also been restored; Art Deco buildings seem especially important in Los Angeles and symbolize the city's optimism and modernity. The fake châteaux that were so popular as instant history in the 1920s are finding admirers as well, and many are benefiting from painstaking restorations now that instant history has become actual history.

Preservation of modest houses, particularly bungalows, is also beginning in the area, though many are being lost to make space for apartment and condominium buildings. Renovation rather than restoration, however, is the most common approach in Los Angeles. In a few places, such as Orange County's La Habra, local banks have made a policy of lending in modest-income areas to preserve bungalows.

It is of a piece with the character of Southern California that real preservation problems persist in public buildings. The ethos of Los Angeles has always been one that has put private before public good. In the architectural development of the region the private house has most often emerged as a work of high art. Though the city has built some fine public build-

A rear view of the Schindler House on N. Kings Road in Hollywood, designed in 1921 for two families and architectural studios. The then-revolutionary design has become a regional classic and is considered the prototype for the countless California patio houses that link interior and garden spaces.

Bungalows both plain and fancy are central to the architectural tradition of Southern California. This massive Craftsman bungalow of the early twentieth century was once threatened with demolition for a street widening along S. Wilton, which the neighborhood fought off. It is now part of a historic district and is undergoing restoration.

In Orange County's La Habra, bungalows such as this row have been rejuvenated through the city-run Neighborhood Housing Services program, which provides financial counseling and home-improvement loans to keep this early tract development of modest-income houses from deteriorating.

ings in the past, many of them (with the exception of City Hall) are insensitively altered and poorly maintained. The public sector doesn't take care of its buildings and shows little pride in them. Even Frank Lloyd Wright's important Hollyhock House in Hollywood's Barnsdall Park was allowed to fall into ruins when it was donated to the city. And when it was restored, the restoration was not in keeping with the cultural importance of the site. Today the superb Streamline Moderne Pan-Pacific Auditorium of 1935, which sits in another public park, is falling into ruin while the city dithers over how to preserve and reuse it. It of all buildings ought to be the easiest to restore and adapt, since only its forward-looking façade needs to be preserved; the rest of the structure is a great barn that could be adapted or replaced. A modern city community center was recently built nearby that could just as easily have been inserted into the landmark—but wasn't.

The Beverly Sycamore on Beverly Boulevard in West Los Angeles is typical of the taste for fantasy in the low-art buildings of the prosperous 1920s. More style than substance, these eggshell-thin stucco châteaux have recently regained their popularity and are being restored by private owners certain they can market the restored building's movie-set charms.

Worst of all is the vandalism that has befallen the monumental Los Angeles Public Library of 1921–1926 in the heart of the booming new high-rise downtown. This major architectural work by Bertram G. Goodhue and Carleton M. Winslow is the most Los Angeles of buildings: a catholic blend of Mediterranean, Roman, Hellenistic, Byzantine, Islamic, and even Egyptian echoes all fused in a stunning Moderne skyscraper of unexpected coherence and power. Inside and out it is enriched with bas-reliefs, mosaics, murals, inscriptions, and custom fittings. In many cities it would be the civic jewel; but to the library board it is merely obsolete. The formal gardens that once led to its front entrance have been paved over for employee parking. In the continuing battle over its future we see the dark side of the Southern California ethos: a crude utilitarianism that sees art as the private luxury of the rich rather than the civic right of society as a whole.

(Top): Before its designation as a historic district, Fifth Avenue lost some historic buildings, demolished to make way for new ones such as this drive-in branch bank. The low-rise bank exposes the sidewall of the district's premier landmark, the turreted Louis Bank of Commerce Building, and shatters the key block's coherence.

The Louis Bank of Commerce Building of 1887, designed by Clements and Stannard at the height of San Diego's railroad-induced boom. After a checkered life, the building was purchased by a San Diego architect who restored it in 1981, replacing the twin wooden turrets that had burned in 1904.

The Romanesque-style Nesmuth-Greely Building was designed by the firm of Comstock and Trotsche in 1888 at the end of San Diego's first boom. When Fifth Avenue declined, its retail and office uses were succeeded by pawnshops, porno stores, and cheap hotels. These uses kept the old building minimally alive.

PORNO AND PRESERVATION: FROM THE STINGAREE TO GASLAMP QUARTER

San Diego, California

SAN Diego, now the second most populous city in California and the eighth in size in the nation, is a classic example of both urban development and urban preservation in the West. Founded as a Spanish colonial outpost in 1769, the first mission in what eventually became the mission chain up the California coast, the city shifted its location in 1868 when a San Francisco capitalist named Alonzo Horton bought 960 acres outside the old town closer to the harbor's deep water and began promoting a "New Town." When a fire swept through the "Old Town" in 1872, this new settlement became all-important. As the early California historian Hubert Howe Bancroft noted, "Every old California town, as it assumes importance, has its 'addition,' which soon becomes the place itself. San Diego, for example, is all 'addition.'"

The earliest preservation efforts in San Diego were, logically enough, in the city's "Old Town." There another San Francisco capitalist, sugar magnate John D. Spreckels, who owned San Diego's streetcar system, bought the crumbling Estudillo adobe in 1905, one of the most elaborate ever built in California, patched it up, renamed it Ramona's Marriage Place (after a popular novel of the period), and promoted tourist travel to the end of his streetcar line. Thus was born a new "Old Town," which eventually became a California state park.

Preservation in the New Town, the center of American San Diego, did not begin until the 1970s.

Alonzo Horton's city, originally focused on the waterfront, saw a gradual shift of prime office development northward. The heart of the Victorian downtown, a substantial brick district built when the Santa Fe Railroad reached San Diego Bay in 1888 and stimulated a boom in the sleepy city, was left behind as fashion and commerce moved into newer buildings north of Broadway. Elaborate Victorian banks, hotels, and fancy stores became pawnshops, low-rent

The foursquare newel post of a Victorian commercial building undergoing restoration on San Diego's once-neglected Fifth Avenue shows the high quality of the city's early buildings.

These new staircases in the Gaslamp Quarter were intended to draw pedestrians into upper floors or down into basements. An ungainly recent addition, they will be removed and the storefront appropriately reconstructed in order to qualify for tax incentives that require accurate restoration.

A neon movie marquee salvaged from another part of town enlivens an indoor food bazaar in a restored Fifth Avenue building.

residential hotels, and bars, and the neighborhood as a whole, in this heavily military city, became a flourishing red-light district known as the Stingaree. Poverty preserved the district as it ran down. Middle-class shoppers avoided the area and it became the home of the city's down-and-out, its drifters, and its many poor pensioners. Prostitution was followed in the 1960s by adult movie theaters and magazine stores. These profitable uses took over the ground floor of old buildings whose upper floors were often sealed off as buildings deteriorated and it became too costly to rehabilitate them.

When San Diego's downtown began booming again in the 1970s, massive redevelopment projects focused investor attention on the old downtown. The upscale Horton Plaza redevelopment project was started adjacent to the new high-rise district and the old Fifth Avenue skid row. Several major department stores and many new small retail stores were planned. Developers launched upper-income housing near the waterfront, thereby creating a new resident shopping population abutting on the old Stingaree. By 1981 at least $14 million in private funds had been poured into the restoration of historic buildings along Fifth Avenue.

The city of San Diego decided that the preservation of Fifth Avenue merited massive public investment as well. Accordingly, in 1976 the city passed

the Gaslamp Quarter Planned District Ordinance to rehabilitate a sixteen-block, thirty-eight-acre strip along Fifth Avenue. In five years, nearly $4 million in public funds was invested in streets, sidewalks, street lamps, landscaping, and other public amenities. Local utilities also contributed toward upgrading the area. In 1980 the district was placed on the National Register. Reducing the number of porno shops was a high priority for the district, and a new city ordinance forbids any new ones from opening. At the same time, however, the city enacted another antipornography ordinance that made it almost impossible for these Fifth Avenue enterprises to move into any other section of the downtown, thereby giv-

New "historic" five-globe streetlights give Fifth Avenue a distinctive look at night. Sidewalk cafés are encouraged to draw more activity into the changing district.

Massive city investments in brick sidewalks and landscaping aim at transforming a down-and-out district into one attractive to San Diegans.

New antipornography legislation has backfired in San Diego. By making new adult shops virtually impossible in other parts of the city, it has encouraged those in the Gaslamp Quarter to make every effort to stay. Now styled "erotic boutiques," many are redesigning their once-garish fronts into pseudo-historic designs such as this one.

One by one the vintage buildings along Fifth Avenue are undergoing restoration. Here a newly restored corner restaurant introduces the process to its block, once lined with pawnshops, porno shops, and bars.

ing them every incentive to stay on as long as they can in their current locations. Once-garish adult shops have remodeled their façades in accordance with new design ordinances, producing more-or-less "historic" porno shops!

The building restorations in the newly christened Gaslamp Quarter have been on the whole quite good. The sidewalk improvements, on the other hand, are overdone. Sidewalk cafés, for example, an excellent idea in San Diego's fine climate, have been permitted to construct permanent barriers on the sidewalks that are unattractive when the café is not in operation. (By contrast, Seattle's Pioneer Square uses movable rope barriers, which are less expensive and less obtrusive, and can be taken in at night, leaving the sidewalk unobstructed.) Some of the new exterior steel staircases added to the fronts of historic buildings to induce retail activity on the second floors were well intentioned but ungainly. A proposed new parking garage, a critically important facility in car-oriented Southern California, is a good idea but a real design challenge.

In the short term the changing district faces several problems. The restoration that has occurred has displaced those who live in residential hotels, forcing destitute people onto the street. Another problem is the great reluctance of San Diegans to think of downtown as a place to linger after hours. Many who work in the gleaming high-rises head home as soon as they leave their offices. For entertainment they are more likely to drive to the beach or the desert or to see a movie in an outlying shopping mall. As a result, many of the pioneer businesses that have revitalized Gaslamp Quarter have had a hard time economically. The rewards have not come as fast as many small investors expected. Restoring buildings is only the first step in restoring vitality to old cities; in the long run, restoring shopping and entertainment patterns is just as important, and even harder.

The Beaux Arts Jeweler's Exchange Building of 1913 was the first tall building in San Diego, built as the downtown moved north up Fifth Avenue. Today it has been refurbished, its ground floor divided into many small jewelry stands.

A large A branded on the ridge overlooking Austin is a characteristic sign of civic pride in the rural West. Here the shape echoes the steeples and finials of this almost-moribund 1860s silver mining town.

DEAD CENTER
IN THE AMERICAN WEST

Austin, Nevada

NOWHERE IS the link between economics and preservation more obvious than in central Nevada. Hubert Howe Bancroft described Austin, Nevada, in 1890 as "that anomaly of modern times, a city in the midst of a wilderness, grown up like a mushroom, in a night." Founded in 1862 when a pony kicked over a rock and uncovered a rich lode of silver ore, the town boomed to ten thousand people in two years. An 1865 account described it as a settlement that "straggles for three miles down a deep, crooked cañon" surrounded by "hundreds of shafts and ditches." It was a city "lying around loose."

Rare, virtually unaltered, one-story commercial buildings line Austin's main street. Canopies over the sidewalks and robust parapets capture the look of the Old West. Most are boarded up or minimally used. Though listed on the National Register of Historic Places, their future is bleak. St. Augustine's Roman Catholic Church of 1866, now sadly run down, greets those who approach the town from the north.

Austin's main street passes up Pony Canyon, where silver was discovered in 1862, resulting in a boom that lured ten thousand people here in two short years. Three impressive red-brick churches (two visible here) dominate the old town. Mobile homes and prefab buildings ring the outskirts, creating a sharp contrast between old and new.

A town of red-brick buildings climbed granite-walled terraces up the steep slopes of the twisting canyon. Along with the county courthouse, Austin boasted three large brick churches—Catholic, Methodist, and Episcopal—that neatly symbolized the principal elements in its bustling population: the Irish, Welsh, and Yankee.

But once the Toiyabe Range had disgorged its silver, an irreversible decline set in. Cattle raising and residual mining kept some life in the town; so did the county courthouse (until it was finally lost to Battle Mountain in 1979). Turquoise mining now pumps some money into the town, but not much. Set square in the center of the state, and almost as far from the interstate highway network as it is possible to be, Austin attracts neither out-of-state gamblers nor many tourists. There is some hunting in the area, and, along with Eureka—a fine old mining town in

a similar situation—Austin attracts Nevadans and other Westerners seeking out historic spots in the Old West. But while this keeps a few motels alive on the fringes, it does little to bring money into the heart of town. So, slowly, Austin decays, and with it one of the finest remaining 1860s settlements in the Old West gradually erodes.

Aggravating the preservation problems of the town is the fact that the few institutions that do have some life in them—the post office, the sheriff's office, the road department, the school district, the local bank, and the turquoise-mining operation—have all chosen to erect nondescript modern buildings rather than buying and restoring the town's historic structures. Especially disturbing is the investment of tax monies in bland new buildings when fine and historically significant old ones stand empty and on the brink of extinction.

St. George Episcopal Church, consecrated in 1878, was paid for by a single passing of the collection plate on Easter Sunday 1877. Recently restored, it continues to function as an Episcopal church.

Granite retaining walls were built as house plots were hacked out of the canyon. This red-brick house with its picket fence and white-painted bays is one of the best-preserved buildings in Austin.

The state of Nevada is not unaware of the architectural significance of Austin; a state survey has pointed out its great importance to the state's heritage, and the town's old buildings have been placed on the National Register of Historic Places. Stokes Castle, outside the town, is even a state landmark. But surveys and designations are not enough; only money can restore and maintain fine old buildings, and here Austin is caught in an iron vise.

Local ignorance also takes its toll. The historic International Hotel, moved piece by piece from Virginia City in 1863 and once the social center of the town, still functions, but its handsome red-brick exterior has been covered over with wood siding to make it look Hollywood Western, and its interior has been "improved" beyond recognition. Building controls are weak to nonexistent; as the local visitors' tabloid puts it, "The people who live in the Austin–Central

Nevada area will tell you that this is the last stronghold of personal freedom in the United States." Rugged individualism makes historic-building-preservation ordinances politically impossible. It is almost a morality play on the theme of short-range individual goals versus the long-range social good, for Austin's sole real asset—now that the mines are gone—is her architectural and townscape heritage. Preserved and cared for, Austin's sagebrush setting, quiet atmo-

Anson P. Stokes, an opulent New York capitalist who owned the Austin Silver Mining Company, built this granite "castle" as a summer house in 1897. Used only that summer, the ruin is now a Nevada state landmark.

sphere, and historic buildings are the only things that could conceivably draw economic activity into this remote spot. So the freedom to alter and destroy in the name of improvement harms not just one building here and there but the whole town's future.

While the overall picture is bleak, a few spots of light cheer the preservationist. Besides its overall townscape, Austin's great treasures are her three brick churches with their bold steeples. St. Augustine's Catholic Church, while dilapidated, is recognized as a historic treasure and the "mother church" of the region for Catholics. The Episcopalian congregation of St. George's has recently restored its church in a sensitive and accurate manner, and the land around it remains undisturbed. Most interesting has been the fate of the Methodist church. Built in 1866, it is as much a monument to creative financing as it is to architecture. Its clever pastor solicited donations of mining stock from his congregation, which he then pooled in the "Methodist Mining Company." Stocks in this corporation were sold back East to build the solid red-brick church. In its heyday it served as both a church and lecture hall. By 1970, however, the old church stood unused. With funds from the Department of the Interior's Heritage Conservation and Recreation Service the building has been carefully restored and a stage was installed inside; the church now serves as a town meeting hall. Paradoxically its death as a church was its salvation as a building, for federal law forbids the use of public money for functioning churches.

Abandoned ranch, Quinn River Valley, Humboldt County: Only the windows were salvaged when the ranch-house was abandoned. It was originally painted white with green trim.

ABANDONED RANCH:
THE LONG-DRAWN-OUT DEATH
OF THE SMALL RANCH

Humboldt County, Nevada

BOTH STOCK raising and agriculture have shared with mining a boom-and-bust character in the West. Rapid development—literally exploitation—has often been quickly followed by abandonment. In the earliest days, when the land was virgin and the native grasses lush, enormous uncontrolled herds of cattle ravaged the open range, denuding the soil and changing the plant ecology forever. Once the native plants were gone, exotic, often noxious weeds invaded the abused ranges. The famous tumbleweed, for example, is a native of Siberia that has become so prevalent in the West that it is now (along with the sagebrush) a symbol for the region.

After cattle came sheep—"hooved locusts," as John Muir branded them—which ate not only the tops of the grasses but the roots of the plants as well, thereby denuding the ranges even more. And farming, almost everywhere else a careful, long-range process of husbandry, was—and to a great degree remains—a virtual mining of the soil or a too-rapid depletion of the water table across the West. In such a situation architectural preservation is superfluous; if the very land is treated as a merely momentary resource, how can any human creation be of much value or concern? The idea that land should be carefully nurtured and buildings built well so that they can be passed down from generation to generation seems alien in much of the American West. The rip-and-run mentality of the miner is the unacknowledged model even for much high-tech agribusiness.

Far northwestern Nevada's Humboldt County, itself larger than five New England states, shows quite sharply the changes that have swept over the sagebrush West. First scoured by miners in the 1860s, it became cattle country by the 1870s, with ranchers from the East, the Midwest, and California as well as immigrants from Germany and Italy. Cattlemen here were farmers as well as livestock producers, with irrigated hayfields and grains raised as feed. The men who work the open range here are called "buck-

Rusting farm machinery lies abandoned in a field in northern Nevada, mute testimony to the rapid changes in technology that have shaped, and then reshaped, the landscape of the American West.

aroos" (from the Spanish *vaquero*), never cowboys. This sparsely settled, arid region reached its population peak about 1900, when small spreads were established wherever the minimally fertile soil would support them. After the cattlemen came merino sheep tended by Basque herders.

The earliest ranch-houses here were built of sod or adobe. Later buildings used local stone (worked by Italian-American masons) and milled lumber brought in by the railroads. Buildings were simple and straightforward, virtually devoid of ornamentation. Lombardy poplar saplings were shipped in as well and planted in straight rows to shade the isolated ranches. After frame building came corrugated metal; and after that, trailer houses and prefabs, today's Western vernacular.

Since the turn of the century big companies have bought out small ranchers and assembled huge tracts. The consolidation of ranches has made many old buildings superfluous. Left to disintegrate, they stand on the landscape as memorials to the fading dream of the small holding. Changing labor patterns have also affected the historical landscape. Today's buckaroos are as likely to be married as single; the bunkhouses that housed the rootless ranch hands have been abandoned in favor of mobile homes and prefabricated houses for small families. Old stone buildings are seen as symbols of poverty and backwardness; little effort is made to preserve or restore them. Granite horse barns are equally obsolete in the age of pickup trucks. Swiftly, the architectural heritage of the American West is disappearing, in part because of genuine improvements in the way West-

The consolidation of ranches and farms in the West into larger units has littered the landscape with "ghost ranches." Here a small frame ranch-house from the first decade of the twentieth century sits between a creaking metal windmill (made in Chicago) and a tall, movable hay derrick.

*Who was Archie Horn? He carefully carved his name into
a beam in the water tower on this remote, lonely ranch.*

*A stone outbuilding, probably built by an Italian
mason, stands next to a square water tower. By the
time the carefully nurtured tree had matured, the
ranch complex was obsolete.*

An old, narrow-clapboard bunkhouse slowly disintegrates on the tawny, treeless land; only its front porch posts and windows were salvaged. Buckaroos today have trailer houses and pickups—the Old West of bunkhouses and horses is a thing of the past.

erners live, and in part through ignorance of the value of the region's architectural past.

Sadly, even prosperous and stable ranches only rarely take an interest in preserving their heritage. The notion of an old homestead to which succeeding generations make reverential additions is irrelevant here. Each generation abandons the house it inherited to build a better modern building, usually totally different from the previous one. Around this new house a wagon-wheel fence, usually brought from somewhere else, makes the house "regional" to its builders. Wealthy ranchers travel to France to see traditional countrysides, never suspecting that their own county could itself have a historical dimension deeper than an old horseshoe nailed over a new stable.

All over the West since the 1960s a fashion for gambrel-roofed "Bavarian" barns that look "historic" has displaced the plain white or red barns that gave the old landscape its particular architectural stamp. Now these quaint styles can be ordered in prefabricated sheet metal with pressed-in "wood grain." Other prosperous Western ranches try to look like Kentucky, another inappropriate model; rarely do Westerners look to their own heritage of simple, unornamented buildings set in plain treescapes of Lombardy poplars or cottonwoods. Real history rots by the roadside: fake history incongruously takes its place. Given this general trend, the preservation of individual old ranches and barns is all the more important. Like the zoos that preserve certain species extinct in the real world, the real American West (not Hollywood's West) may someday survive only in county historical society compounds rather than in its original, evocative settings.

An old-fashioned corral made of random posts and woven brush stands empty. Today's fences and corrals are made of thin steel posts with barbed wire strung across them as tightly as guitar strings.

VANISHING ZION: GREAT BASIN MORMONDOM'S FARM VILLAGES

Sanpete County and Spring City, Utah

SANPETE County, Utah, is the last and best treasury of a singular achievement in the American West: the centrally planned Great Basin Mormon landscape. One hundred miles south of booming Salt Lake City, mercifully bypassed by Interstate 15, lost behind the Wasatch Range, this now-stagnant agricultural valley and its string of Mormon villages is a vanishing national treasure.

Unlike all other Western settlements, those in the "Mormon Corridor," a great swath from southern Idaho through Utah and into Nevada and Southern California, were the result of a planned, centrally controlled colonization. There was no building free-for-all here as in almost all the rest of the West. Beliefs, society, and economy were all directed by church leaders, who first picked a settlement leader

The great Manti Temple dominates the San Pitch River Valley, one of the last intact old Mormon landscapes. Built from stone quarried from the yellow limestone bluff it crowns, the impregnable temple seems to leap up to confront the granite Wasatch Range.

The Gothic revival Spring City Meetinghouse was designed by Richard C. Watkins of Provo and erected between 1900 and 1914 by skilled Danish and American masons. Threatened by demolition because some thought it obsolete, it was saved by Bishop Osral Allred and the people of Spring City, who added a new wing in 1973 built of the same stone as the original chapel.

(Opposite): The splendid Manti Temple in Sanpete County fuses Gothic revival and Second Empire elements in a castlelike whole designed by William H. Folsom and erected by the Latter-Day Saints between 1877 and 1888. Set in a mature, irrigated landscape, it is an outstanding symbol of an American Zion planted in the vast Great Basin.

This dry ditch and row of willows epitomizes the key to the design of the traditional Mormon landscape: irrigation systems that dictated how fields were divided and where and what form settlement took. Today more efficient sprinklers are replacing the murmuring ditches.

Many barns in the West are painted white or red, but Mormon barns and fences are traditionally left unpainted. Here an open-sided hay barn, with its roof gone, weathers away in the heart of Spring City. Farmers traditionally do not pull down old buildings, nor do they burn old relics.

and a balanced assortment of colonists, then chose the general area if not the specific site for settlement, and finally provided both financing and what amounted to a complete city-planning code.

In contrast to the typical isolated American farmstead surrounded by fields and miles from its neighbors, the Church of Jesus Christ of Latter-Day Saints imposed a planned Zion of what geographers call "nucleated villages." Farmers walked out to their fields each day but came home to socially dense settlements at night. This intensified community life and created an open countryside of grid-patterned fields and relatively compact small towns.

The all-pervasive American gridiron town plan was developed in a distinctive way here that still stamps certain settlements in the West as Mormon founded. Every square seven-acre block was subdivided into large lots, each a farmstead with a house in front and various barns and service buildings in back. Houses—at first small log cabins or adobe structures—were built on the corners of the blocks. What pulled all these farmsteads together was a centralized system of irrigation ditches. Located where the sidewalk would be in other towns, narrow irrigation channels lie across the path to every house. There is the constant happy murmur of water here in the high desert. Some commentators have seen an archaic purity in Mormon town-building: the reestablishment of the New England village. These were, however, improved villages—absolutely geometric, with none of the geographic irregularities so characteristic of New England settlements.

The Eastern-born Latter-Day Saints carried traditional Northeastern house types in their memories when they migrated west. These they re-created in their new Zion. Two-story, central-hall houses were especially popular. In Utah, the symmetrical, central-hall house is often called a "Nauvoo-style house," a "polygamy house," or just a "Mormon house." (Actually, most polygamous husbands kept separate houses for each wife and family.)

In Sanpete County's Spring City, located off rather than on state highway 89, this traditional pattern, eroded away almost everywhere else, still holds on by the skin of its teeth. Originally Spring Town, it was established as a frontier Mormon outpost with a fort in 1853. A year later the Utes burned the fort and drove the Mormons from the area, but in 1859 the Mormons resettled the valley permanently. They surveyed the land, dug irrigation ditches, and raised abundant crops; the area became the breadbasket of Utah. A quarry was opened south of the town and, with its honey-colored limestone, handsome houses, barns, a meetinghouse, and other buildings were constructed. The prosperity that came to this valley after the introduction in the 1880s of merino and rambouillet sheep, whose fine wool fetched good prices, was expressed in a wave of solid masonry con-

Only in the Mormon West were separate farmsteads built in town clusters rather than scattered across the landscape. Here a Spring City Greek revival farmhouse on its original large lot stands paired with its old, weathered barn. Beyond both is another frame farmhouse with its open-sided hay barn.

Some prosperous farmers built stone barns, which have weathered to a warm yellow. The barns behind the Jacob Johnson house in Spring City stand in an old apple orchard; in the foreground is a typical "Mormon fence" of random boards.

Jacob Johnson, a lawyer, built a twin-chimney stone house in 1875, the gable end of which is seen to the left. When he became a circuit judge in the 1890s he added the massive Queen Anne wing with its round tower.

struction. This turned out to be the high point for architecture in rural Mormondom. Styles were conservative: the meetinghouse, built as late as 1900–1914 in the Gothic revival style, looks as if it could be sixty years older.

In many other countries, or even in other parts of the West, Sanpete County's rich architectural past would be its present and future as well. Travelers interested in American history and the many Mormons who come to Salt Lake City today would, after seeing Temple Square in Zion's capital, make a pilgrimage to Mormondom's rural roots. But neither the changing Mormon church nor very many individual Mormons have been concerned with the preservation of their noteworthy past. Superb buildings such as the splendid Coalville Tabernacle have been demolished for bland, if functional, replacements. The famous temple and tabernacle in Salt Lake City are dwarfed today by a new high-rise church headquarters. And in Spring City the small but contextually important commercial district was torn down when the man who owned most of its buildings heard that they might be made landmarks! Even the eternal-looking temple in nearby Manti (built 1877–1888) is threatened with insensitive "renovation" that would spoil one of the finest creations of Mormon culture.

Countering this melancholy trend is the work of organizations such as Utah Heritage Foundation and

Many contemporary additions to old stone buildings in Spring City spoil the architectural quality of historic structures. Judge Johnson's law office and court, a warm yellow limestone building of perfect proportions, has recently had an ungainly gray cinder-block wing added.

Some people, often Mormons from elsewhere, recognize the quality of Spring City's old houses. This solid, light-yellow brick house of about 1910 was bought by a potter and a stained-glass artist, who are restoring and expanding it. The new wing to the right is built with bricks made from the same clay as the old house.

Local people tend to see stone houses as symbols of poverty. On the left the Endowment House, built in 1876, was permitted to decay, even though it is one of the most important structures in Spring City. A Salt Lake City artist has bought the old relic and propped up the collapsing corner, and will restore it as a studio and home. The stone house to the right has recently been restored with a fancy bargeboard added.

of the state of Utah itself, which are trying to change the attitudes of the Mormon church and of local building owners who consider their vintage buildings impediments to "progress." It is an uphill struggle.

Spring City has recently passed a zoning law—the first of its type in rural Utah—to forestall the subdivision of the old lots that would destroy the town's historic Mormon pattern. Future battles loom over the uncontrolled placement of mobile homes, which could equally impair the character of the town.

In an ideal world, the entire upper San Pitch River Valley would be declared a national historic landscape and any future changes and legitimate improvements would be sensitively worked into the historic fabric. A line would be drawn at Spanish Fork, south of Provo, beyond which strip development would be prohibited. Fine historic buildings would be restored, not "renovated," and efforts would be made to get Mormons in particular to visit this quiet valley that still contains so much of their singular heritage. This would spur local pride and the understanding among owners of old buildings that they possess treasures central to Mormon—and American—history. More than just a few historic structures should be saved here. The whole flavor of this utopian landscape is important.

The robust, red-brick Spring City Public School of 1899 was designed by Richard C. Watkins and built with bricks made in the town brickyard. The twin chimneys, pulled together and flanking the central flagpole, echo the twin chimneys at the opposite ends of traditional central-hall houses. It is a remarkable testimony to the high regard Spring City had for its public buildings. Unwanted, the Spring City Public School was sold for one dollar to the Daughters of the Utah Pioneers in 1959. Beyond the 1899 school is the 1916 junior high, and beyond it, the metal prefabs of the present-day school system. The trio tells the sad story of the rise, decline, and fall of public architecture in rural Utah.

Rugged Telegraph Hill rises behind remote Silver City, a wooden mining town that flourished in the 1860s. The town survives as a quiet summer resort for history-conscious Westerners. Shiny corrugated-metal roofs protect the surviving buildings from the heavy winter snows.

HISTORIC MINING TOWN:
THE REAL THING

Silver City, Idaho

SILVER City has a name that rings as clear as a silver cartwheel. A wooden boomtown built in a narrow valley in Idaho's wild Owyhee Mountains when gold and silver were discovered there in May 1863, it died when the mines closed in 1875 following the failure of the Bank of California in San Francisco. In 1890 there was a brief revival of the mines and the town, but this second boomlet was soon over. Silver City's people moved on, seeking work. The town wasted away. Neglect and fire destroyed building after building. The heavy snows of each severe winter crushed those buildings whose roofs were not maintained.

Silver City remained the seat of Owyhee County, and this drew a trickle of local people into the dying town, but when irrigation opened the Snake River Valley to agriculture, the low country became the new center of population. More houses and stores disappeared as they were sold, dismantled, and carted away to be used for building material in the valley. When the county seat was removed to Murphy, out of the mountains and on the highway, in 1935, the town's last economic prop collapsed. The Granite Block, the finest building in town, which had been turned into the Owyhee County Court House, was sold and torn down for salvage, leaving parts of its façade's stone arcade as a melancholy ruin.

During World War II the rationing of tires and gasoline stopped all but the most essential travel to the remote town. The local power company removed the electrical system to salvage the copper in the wires, and the town reverted to kerosene

Wildflowers bloom in Silver City's cemetery, which freezes the nineteenth-century social structure of the town in elevation and stone. Wrought- and cast-iron fences imported from St. Louis or Salt Lake City still protect the graves of the town's well-to-do. This hand, book, and rose decorate a Silver City tombstone of 1896 in the Lodge Cemetery.

lamps. Silver City became a ghost of its former self. More buildings collapsed or were torn down. The population dwindled down to a single man, Willie Hawes, a self-appointed guardian who stayed through the severe winters. When spring came, opening the road and letting in visitors, he protected its buildings. In the 1940s the town was publicized as a ghost town and Willie Hawes became an Idaho celebrity.

During the 1950s Westerners exploring their own

Buckaroos drive "critters" through Silver City. Owyhee County became a vast rangeland by the 1880s. Today, while nearly all the mines have long since closed, ranching continues in this far corner of the West.

region by automobile discovered Silver City, and a revival slowly started in the remnants of the town. People from Boise, other parts of Idaho, and other Western states bought the surviving buildings and fixed them up as summer cottages. Galvanized metal roofs and shutters of recycled wood have been the salvation of Silver City's old buildings. The original roofs were of wooden shingles, but today all the buildings in the town are protected by less expensive, more durable metal roofs that resist fire and shed snow. The bright silver color of fresh roofs means that the delicate structures are being preserved.

Discovery of this quaint relic also brought everyone from antique buyers to bottle hounds to plain looters. Buildings were shuttered during the winter, but that was not enough. The Silver City Taxpayers' Association had to be formed to hire a deputized watchman to guard the town from visitors who hiked in or, today, roar in on snowmobiles. The most prominent sign in Silver City stands at its entrance and proclaims in large letters: **WELCOME TO SILVER CITY, IDAHO. ALL PROPERTY IS PRIVATELY OWNED.**

The largest building in Silver City is the rambling Idaho Hotel on Jordan Street, built in 1866 and expanded several times. The peaked roof that pops up over the hotel was recently added to prevent winter snows from crushing the fragile structure. The boarded-up building next door was once the hotel's annex, and before that the Idaho Exchange. An old flag flies from the porch. The hotel survives because of the love of its dedicated proprietor, Ed Jagels. Those with sleeping bags can camp out in its unrestored rooms—a singular experience.

A rusted corrugated-steel roof protects an old Silver City house now used only occasionally.

(Below): Knapp's Drug Store, built in 1896, has ornament made from small pieces of wood nailed together, an economical way of copying the carved and turned wooden decorations of wealthy cities such as San Francisco.

PLEASE DO NOT DESTROY OR TRESPASS. VIOLATORS WILL BE PROSECUTED. OWYHEE COUNTY SHERIFF. Attached to this sign is another sign that warns: **NO DIGGING ON TOWN PROPERTY.** These signs are the first line of defense against relic hunters who have stripped Western ghost towns that are not protected.

Preservation in Silver City is changing. Early preservation was a kind of collage: pieces or furnishings were taken from semiruined buildings to make the sounder buildings livable as summer houses. Old boards were cut to make shutters, holes were patched over with whatever old material came to hand. Many of Silver City's buildings are now jigsaw puzzles of old boards, which has a charm of its own.

Today Silver City is listed on the National Register, and county building controls prohibit inappropriate buildings. Since the Idaho Hotel and the Schoolhouse Museum are virtually the only commerce in town, it preserves its unique, quiet atmosphere. New structures must be of wood and have wooden, not metal, window sashes. There is no gas station in town, and, except for a very few telephone wires, virtually no sign of the twentieth century. The streets remain unpaved. The federal Bureau of Land Management owns the surrounding countryside, protecting the historic town's unspoiled setting, which is as important as the town itself.

(Opposite): This row of buildings on Washington Street shows both early and contemporary preservation in Silver City. The two buildings on the right exemplify the relaxed, funky, collagelike preservation that evolved in the 1950s as old buildings were recycled. On the left, spiffy in its fresh white paint, is the old meat market, which typifies the more accurate contemporary preservation, when an effort is made to bring buildings back to their original appearance.

Much of the charm of Silver City is due to the "natural" way that fragments from buildings or old iron machinery lie scattered around. When buildings fall they are left as ruins rather than cleared away. Still without electricity, Silver City gives a unique impression at night, when two or three kerosene lamps glow yellow in the darkened town. Unromantic as it might seem, though, the restoration of electricity would greatly reduce the hazard of fire and help preserve the town.

Key buildings in Silver City are preserved by groups based elsewhere in the state. The white-frame Our Lady of Tears church, built in 1896, was sold by the Episcopal Church to the Roman Catholic

Willie Hawes's sidewalk stand next to the meat market uses bits and pieces picked up from all over town. Such early preservation efforts, while not authentic or historic, have their own whimsical charm.

More sophisticated restorations take place in Silver City now that county landmark ordinances protect the National Register town. The Getchell Drug Store had its porch rebuilt and the rest of the building brought back from near ruin. Upstairs is a summer apartment, downstairs a private museum filled with old drugstore goods and paraphernalia.

Diocese of Boise, which uses it for occasional summer masses. The state's Masonic lodges as a group preserve the large wooden Masonic Hall that straddles Jordan Creek. Idaho's members of the Independent Order of Odd Fellows collectively preserve their 1870s hall. And the Owyhee County Cattlemen's Association leases and preserves the 1892 schoolhouse; its second floor serves as the town's museum. Silver City is indeed lucky to be loved by so many Idahoans.

Today some houses in Silver City are being thoroughly restored in a much more accurate way. The contrast is quite remarkable; here and there, a house with spanking fresh paint pops out from a cluster of warmly weathered neighbors. Preservation here is a slow turnaround toward the normal upkeep and repainting that living buildings need. Building by building, summer house owners are taking better care of their properties. Silver City has come back from the brink of extinction.

But one rip-roaring fire could sweep it all away.

Silver City's antique water system, an open wooden vat fed by hillside springs, is being replaced by a buried metal tank. A modern water system will increase the town's odds against its nemesis: fire.

An 1860s house undergoing extensive restoration, including a new coat of white paint. The old ghost town has returned from the brink of extinction.

(Opposite): In Silver City, it might be said that intoxication furthered education, since tax revenue from its many saloons funded the public school. The town's second small boom paid for this large wooden school of 1892. A touch of classical erudition was given to the building by the pressed-metal pediments placed over the windows. In 1960, the Owyhee County Cattlemen's Association restored the building. The first floor is now used for the cattlemen's annual July convention; the second floor houses a private museum assembled by the county's remarkable local historian, Mildretta Adams.

Built as a planing mill spanning Jordan Creek, this large building became Silver City's Masonic Hall; the compass and square insignia was etched into the window in the pediment. A few years ago every Mason in Idaho was asked to contribute to a fund to shore up the venerable lodge.

Visible beyond a recently restored house is the white-frame church built in 1896 as an Episcopalian chapel. In 1928, when that congregation dwindled, the church was sold to the Catholic Diocese of Boise, which rededicated it Our Lady of Tears. It is used for occasional masses during the summer months.

Expectations of the extension of the Oregon and California Railroad to Jacksonville led to the construction of the United States Hotel, begun in 1879 and completed in 1881 by Jeanne DeRoboam Holt. By the 1940s it was rundown but still in operation, housing the town library as well as the hotel itself. In the early 1960s the Siskiyou Pioneer Sites Foundation was organized, and it and the Lions Club promoted the restoration of the hotel's balcony. The restoration was completed in 1965 with the support of the U.S. National Bank of Oregon, which made an advance payment on a ten-year lease and opened a branch on the ground floor furnished with local antiques.

COPING WITH SUCCESS: PRESERVATION, COMMUNITY, AND TOURISM

Jacksonville, Oregon

JACKSONVILLE is that rarest of places: a historic town whose residents mobilized to preserve its many fine buildings and which has then adjusted to an influx of visitors without spoiling its rare charm. It stands as a model for small-town preservation in the West.

During the winter of 1851–1852, gold was discovered in Rich Gulch near Jackson Creek in southern Oregon. Miners from California rushed to the "fresh diggin's" and set up camp there. The settlement went through the usual Western boomtown evolution of canvas tents, hastily built frame buildings, and then, after a series of fires, sturdier brick structures. When the placer mines were played out, agriculture spread through the valley. In 1860, the town of Jacksonville was formally incorporated. It became the county seat, which made it the regional center of commerce and activity. After a number of devastating fires in the 1870s, ordinances were passed that mandated the use of brick along the main street.

Geography dictated that the Oregon and California Railroad, later the Southern Pacific, be built in the valley away from the town. To forestall a shift of the county seat out of Jacksonville and into the valley, the town built a grand new courthouse in the Italianate style in 1883. The 1880s were Jacksonville's peak. Commercial property boomed. But the construction of the courthouse, and of the Rogue River Valley Railway, which linked the town with the main line at Medford, did not stem the town's decline. The final blow came in 1927, when the town lost the county seat to rival Medford.

Fruit raising and a minimum of local commerce

The Jackson County Court House in Jacksonville was built in 1883 in the Italianate style. In 1927, the county seat was moved to Medford and the old building was closed. In 1948, county voters approved a tax for historical purposes and in 1950 the Southern Oregon Historical Society reopened the courthouse as the county museum. It became the nucleus for the preservation of the red-brick town.

kept the settlement from becoming a ghost town, while poverty kept it from changing. Pride in the town's history also developed among some of its residents. C. C. Beekman's bank, closed in 1912, was left undisturbed. Four decades later the Siskiyou Pioneer Sites Foundation stepped in to save Beekman's house and Victorian furnishings, which his family had preserved. The house of pioneer photographer Peter Britt, who had thoroughly documented the town in its heyday, was preserved intact by his children. (Unfortunately, the house burned in 1957, but by then Britt's precious glass negatives had been safely stored in the county museum.)

In 1950, using tax money voted by the county for historical purposes, the old Jacksonville courthouse was opened as a museum by the Southern Oregon Historical Society. In 1953, the town was described in the *Journal of the Society of Architectural Historians,* and more people became aware of its historic value. Fights over a proposed highway that would have sliced through the town's historic residential area, and later over urban-renewal plans, further galvanized the citizenry. Under the leadership of such

This corner of California Street burned in 1884 and was immediately rebuilt. The large building housed the meeting hall of the Improved Order of Redmen, a fraternal organization whose members were mostly of German descent. Its 1940s neon J-VILLE TAVERN sign has been preserved.

When Pacific Northwest Bell needed new facilities in Jacksonville it built this arcaded, red-brick building catercorner from the Masonic Hall. Inside the arcade is a show-window museum of old telephone equipment. The modern streetlights reproduce the town's historic lamps. Next door to the phone company is the red-brick post office, built in 1968, which picks up the theme of the arches seen in the town's historic structures. The peaked-roof building, built in 1891 as the Rogue River Valley Railway depot, serves as the Jacksonville Chamber of Commerce's visitor information center.

At the other end of this key California Street block stands the Masonic Hall, built in 1875. A motif of ground-floor arches unifies all the buildings on the block.

The north side of California Street, between Third and Oregon, was built up between 1856 and the mid-1870s with one-story brick stores. An unhistoric pair of frame in-fill buildings have recently been added to the row. Across the intersection is the arcade of the new phone company building.
While tolerable from a distance, the two contemporary frame buildings on California Street disrupt the architecture of the town's main street when seen up close. The unpainted Bella Union on the left was built in 1970 for a movie and strains hard to be Old West, though with a picture window. The painted structure to its right was built in 1982 over protests from local preservationists, who pointed out that Jacksonville had never had a building like it.

local men as Robertson Collins and such institutions as the U.S. National Bank of Oregon, more and more residents came to feel that Jacksonville's past was its future.

In 1967, more than a hundred nineteenth-century buildings in the town were placed on the National Register of Historic Places. Eventually several small museums opened, and antique shops and restaurants have blossomed along the old main street. A historic preservation commission and a design approval commission were established; both were later combined in the citywide Historical and Architectural Review Commission. The phone company and the post office built compatible buildings in the revived Jacksonville in the 1960s, showing that the town could accommodate needed improvements without destroying its character. People now live in Jacksonville and work in nearby Medford. The annual Peter Britt Music and Arts Festival, begun in 1963, gives added luster to the town each August. Jacksonville has achieved what seems almost impossible in the rest of the West: conservation with growth, preservation with revitalization, change without destruction.

Portland emerged as the metropolis of the
nineteenth-century Pacific Northwest. Rows of
substantial brick and cast-iron commercial buildings
lined the streets parallel to the wharves.
(Right): 111–113 S.W. Front Street,
built in 1872, is a rare survivor from the period.
(Above): This sill and drain from one of S.W. Front
Street's rare survivors from the 1870s show
the quality of Portland's early, and now mostly
lost, cast-iron architectural heritage.
(Top right): Pieces of Portland's cast-iron heritage are
scattered through the modern city. This pathetic
ruin attempted to recycle cast-iron architectural elements in a failed 1960s restaurant.

FRAGMENTED HERITAGE:
STITCHING TOGETHER A RAVAGED CITY

Portland, Oregon

BIG CITIES with a continuous record of growth have been those least mindful of the value of architectural preservation, at least until recent years. Portland, the major metropolis of the Pacific Northwest throughout the nineteenth century, had an exceedingly rich architectural heritage in its public buildings, parks, churches, and commercial district. Along with lower Manhattan and St. Louis's riverfront, it boasted the greatest concentration of cast-iron commercial buildings in the nation. Situated at the head of navigation of the Willamette River, near its junction with the Columbia, Portland was strategically placed to serve as the outlet for the agricultural riches of Oregon's fertile Willamette Valley. When New York financier Henry Villard's Northern Pacific Railroad reached Portland in 1883, the city's regional dominance was assured. Four transcontinental rail systems focused on Portland by the first decade of the twentieth century.

While Portland has followed the national economic patterns of cyclical growth and stagnation, whenever there *has* been growth in Oregon, it has been here. Today it remains the most important city in the state. In 1890 it was the seventh largest city west of the Mississippi, while Seattle was ninth. By 1980 Portland was sixteenth while Seattle remained ninth. Still, Portland has seen much building over the last twenty years. As modern Portland grew, the center of its downtown office district shifted south. The 1870s cast-iron downtown along the river was left behind as Skid Row. In the 1930s this old district received its heaviest blow, when most of the build-

ings east of S.W. Front Street were demolished to build a seawall and U.S. 99 along the riverfront. That badly sited "improvement" was in turn made obsolete when the interstate highway was built on the other, industrial, side of the river. Today part of the 1930s highway right-of-way has been planted with grass and trees and made into a pleasant riverfront park. Few know that its open lawns (which could be

When construction of the new interstate highway across the river made the 1930s highway obsolete, Waterfront Park was developed on the site of the old cast-iron row. Visible in the center of the photo is the top of 111–113 S.W. Front Street; between the two tallest high-rises is Michael Graves's new Postmodern Portland Public Service Building.

Preservation? The 1951 Central Fire Station on S.W. Front Street awkwardly mounted pieces of demolished cast-iron buildings on the wall that masks its parking lot.

The superb Gothic revival Bishop's House, built of brick and cast iron at 219–223 S.W. Stark Street, has recently been restored with a new ground-floor restaurant. Next door is one of the old district's ubiquitous parking lots.

anywhere) were once the site of their city's first great architectural achievement.

As the downtown shifted, buildings in the discarded old downtown were cleared away for parking lots. Fire claimed others, land speculation still more. It became much more profitable, and vastly easier, for a landlord to tear down an old, decayed-through-neglect firetrap, lease the land to a parking-lot company, and simply collect a check each month. Even if a building owner wanted to do major work on his building, it was unlikely that any bank would have found it a prudent thing to lend money for. The erosion of the old city has been substantial; in many places in the old districts, at least every other half-block is an unsightly, if useful, parking lot. Few parts of any old streets have not been visually blasted by this inefficient, wasteful, but cheap and profitable shift in land use.

In the past, Portland thought of preservation in terms of isolated public monuments (such as its fine and treasured city hall and courthouse) rather than of its old commercial district or its streetscapes. But in 1975, Oregon's state legislature (in Salem, not Portland) passed legislation granting a fifteen-year

(Above): The burned-out shell of an 1870s building at 124 Yamhill Street in a National Register district shows more than one layer of history. When it is restored, no doubt its ground floor—redesigned in the 1960s—will be brought back closer to its nineteenth-century appearance.

(Left): The successor to brick and cast iron was brick and rough sandstone. The façade of the 1892 Simon Building was left standing after a fire gutted it in 1970; it now masks a parking lot while maintaining a sense of continuity along the street.

(Below): Here at S.W. First and Ash streets a handsome old building with large plate-glass windows is up for lease. In front of it is a modern streetlight that is both contemporary in feeling and appropriate to its historic setting.

property-tax freeze for historic properties that are appropriately rehabilitated. This statewide policy has had a good effect on Portland. The city-administered Urban Conservation Loan Fund also makes some loans available for restoration, using federal Community Development Block Grants and diminishing urban-renewal funds.

In Portland's ravaged riverside commercial district, what remains is now being restored. The great challenge is designing good in-fill buildings in the gaps that scar the historic city. Whereas in the nineteenth century buildings in the congested downtown were built in four or five walk-up stories, today regulations are required to force developers to build even two stories, since the common wisdom is that shoppers will not climb even one flight up (and escalators, for most stores, are prohibitively expensive). Twentieth-century shoppers expect a degree of convenience and ease that nineteenth-century city people did not dream of. In addition, the old arrangement of mixed uses, with shops on the lower floors and offices and residences above, is no longer a natural pattern in modern America. Retailers and restaurateurs want large, one-story buildings, while office buildings (with elevators) tend to be five, ten, or more stories, with banks occupying their ground levels, not retail operations. In Portland's historic districts the compromise between modern uses and older cityscape patterns has been to construct large, two-story buildings whose façades are broken down into units echoing the older, narrow shop fronts. Inside, these large buildings are divided into mini-malls. This seems the best compromise possible for twentieth-century building in nineteenth-century districts.

The two-story Yamhill Marketplace, under construction in 1982, breaks up its ground floor into the traditional module of small shop fronts, even though its interior is one large, subdivided retail space.

The white terra-cotta-clad Jackson Tower of 1910 at 806 S.W. Broadway in Portland's theater district, a fine example of Beaux Arts skyscraper design, has recently been restored. Across the street is the Fox Theater, with its flamboyant neon sign.

Nineteenth-century Portland was notable for the high quality of its public buildings. That tradition has been revived today in Michael Graves's Portland Public Service Building. Its colorful Postmodern design makes a wry reference to neoclassical architecture with its overscaled motif of two "columns" with projecting capitals supporting a large "keystone."

The octagonal, copper-roofed Crown Point Vista House of 1917 commands a sweeping view of the dramatic Columbia River Gorge. It is the architectural capstone of highway engineer Samuel C. Lancaster's pioneering Columbia River Scenic Highway, opened in 1915.

MONUMENTS OF
THE EARLY AUTOMOTIVE LANDSCAPE

The Columbia River Scenic Highway,
Multnomah Falls Lodge,
and St. John's Bridge, Oregon

WHILE THE automobile brought destruction into the heart of many of the West's historic cities in the form of sprawling parking lots and disruptive highways, here and there—especially in the parkways of the early twentieth century and the great bridges of the 1930s—the automobile has occasioned the creation of some of the most distinctively American monuments on the modern landscape. Today the best of these achievements have become historic treasures presenting special preservation problems of their own. At the majestic 1937 Golden Gate Bridge in San Francisco, often cited as the most popular man-made landmark in the West, the streamlined Art Deco toll booths were recently slated to be replaced with ugly boxes. Only after public pressure did the bridge district's governing commission scrap that insensitive plan and hire an architect to design new and compatible booths.

Oregon has been more respectful of its early automotive heritage. The superb Columbia River Scenic Highway, the earliest and arguably still the most beautiful scenic highway in the West, has recently been the object of a historical and engineering survey, the first step in its preservation. Built between 1912 and 1915, it was the first major asphalt highway in the Northwest. But its real importance lies in having raised engineering to the level of an environmental art, making the highway an asset to the landscape, not just a gash through it. Engineer Samuel C. Lancaster aligned the road to reveal the colossal basaltic gorge's scenic qualities to their best advantage, making a drive on his road a constantly unfurling revelation of nature's wonders. "On starting the surveys," he wrote, "our first business was to find the beauty spots, or those points where the most beautiful things along the line might be seen to best advantage, and if possible to locate the road in such a way as to reach them." The design of the road's individual elements saw the same concern for aesthetics. Graceful stone bridges, viaducts, masonry walls, and windowed tunnels made every part of the highway a work of art. Only indigenous rock was used, so that the highway structures blend with their setting. Designed for smaller, slower automobiles, the highway makes the landscape more immediate, from the trees along its edge to the waterfalls in the distance.

Late in the 1940s, a wider, faster, river-level highway (now Interstate 84) was built parallel to the Columbia River Scenic Highway (designated U.S. 30 after 1921). The existence of the newer road preserved the older one as a road for leisurely automobile touring. With the Multnomah Falls Lodge as a way station and the rustic, WPA-built Timberline Lodge of 1935–1938 as a destination, the highway preserves an important chapter in the development of modern America: the birth of the automotive highway age.

Few roads are as self-consciously artistic as the Columbia River Scenic Highway, but quite a few of the West's bridges are. The bridges and other public works of the 1930s were carefully styled monuments on the land. The stylistically conservative, but nonetheless beautifully designed, St. John's Bridge outside Portland, Oregon, is a good example. Its steel

At Multnomah Falls, fourth highest falls in the West, the city of Portland built the Multnomah Falls Lodge in 1925 as a rest stop along the Columbia River Scenic Highway. A property of the U.S. Forest Service since 1943, the lodge has recently been improved; the three bay windows are new additions.

piers leap straight up, belying their great weight and strength. Such fine works should be looked *at* as well as looked *from.* The development of a small park and boat landing underneath the bridge's approach ramp is a clever use of a dramatic space.

Some of the West's great dams, bridges, and other public works are among the greatest designs and biggest structures in the nation. Their conservation and enhancement is a key part of preservation in the future.

Highway engineer Samuel C. Lancaster sought to make his scenic highway blend with its magnificent setting. Retaining walls, bridges, and viaducts were faced with local granite laid by skilled Italian-American masons. Today these fragile works deserve careful restoration rather than mere replacement.

The apple-green St. John's Bridge of 1931 spanning the Willamette River was designed by David Steinman in the Gothic style. Steinman sought to "preach the gospel of beauty in steel"; his romantic design was both economical and artistic. Recently a park was developed under the pointed arches of the bridge's approach ramp.

In the distance is the Osborn house of 1873, recently reroofed with the assistance of the Washington State Office of Archaeology and Historic Preservation and a Department of the Interior grant. The new house in the foreground fuses traditional shapes and materials with contemporary elements.

ONE HAMLET AND ONE FAMILY

Oysterville, Washington

Onlly rarely is preservation due to the continued activity of succeeding descendants of the original builders. Located at the tip of the Long Beach Peninsula embracing Willapa Bay, Oysterville was settled in 1854 by I. A. Clarke and R. H. Espy, who came to harvest the rich beds of native oysters for the lucrative Gold Rush–era San Francisco market. But by the late 1880s, when the oyster beds were depleted, the once-thriving settlement had shrunk dramatically. Today Oysterville is a sleepy hamlet.

This history of boom and bust is not exceptional in the West, but the continuing interest of the Espy family in the town they helped found is. While the town dwindled down to a handful of buildings, the grandchildren of W. H. Espy held on to their old-fashioned houses. They also preserved their interest in the old Baptist church, which Espy had given to the town in 1892. A small, nonprofit foundation was formed to restore the long-unused church, and with the help of the Washington State Office of Archaeology and Historic Preservation and a matching grant-in-aid from the National Park Service, the intimate church with its gaily shingled steeple was meticulously restored. The entire hamlet was placed on the National Register of Historic Places, in order to preserve not just its surviving buildings but its undisturbed setting as well.

Today the hamlet of Oysterville is a mixture of year-round residents, a few of whom still work the

This Gothic revival clapboard house of 1869 is named Tsako-te-hahsh-eet, the old Native American name for this area, "land of the red-top grass and home of the woodpecker." The house continues to be painted a conservative white with green trim; its garden is vivid with dahlias and roses.

now-seeded oyster beds of Willapa Bay, and summer people, some from Portland. After driving through the string of beach towns strung out along the peninsula, arriving at the end of the road in Oysterville feels like stepping back in time and geography to nineteenth-century New England. The misty estuary, with its wisps of low-lying vapor, stretches out gray and motionless, much like similar places in Massachusetts or Rhode Island. A desire to keep what remains of the past permeates the town. The 1940s oyster plant—anywhere else likely to be thought an eyesore to be ripped down—is here a treasured link with the past, a sign of continuity, and a place still used to shuck oysters.

(Above): The simple Oysterville School of 1907, long since superseded by modern schools in larger towns nearby, has been preserved and converted into the town's community hall.

(Left and below): The Oysterville Baptist Church of 1892, a gift to his town from founder R. H. Espy, was inactive by the 1930s. The old building, no longer a house of worship, was restored with funds authorized by the Historic Preservation Act of 1966.

Shells litter the ground at the oyster-shucking plant. The
inclined trough at the right housed a conveyor belt that carried
the shellfish into the now minimally active plant.

Oysterville's plain clapboard houses stand between the flat coastal
marshes and the pine forests of its peninsula. Devoid of unnecessary
"improvements," the sleepy hamlet is happy simply not to change.

A detail of foliage and masks from the Richardsonian Jefferson County Courthouse of 1892, designed by Willis A. Ritchie of Seattle. Begun just as the railroad-inspired boom peaked, the monumental courthouse still serves as the seat for one of the Olympic Peninsula's two huge but sparsely populated counties. Constructed of hard red brick imported from St. Louis, this is one of the two oldest courthouses in Washington State.

BOOM, BUST, AND PRESERVATION

Port Townsend, Washington

S PECTACULARLY SITED on the northeast tip of the forested Olympic Peninsula, where the Strait of Juan de Fuca meets Admiralty Inlet, Port Townsend was platted out in 1852 and boomed in 1889 and 1890. Located where the almost constant westerly winds of the strait met the calmer waters of the sound, Port Townsend was ideally situated for sailing vessels. But when steamers became dominant, it was bypassed in favor of Seattle. Expectations that it would become the terminus of the transcontinental railroad led to a frantic real estate and building boom, and impressive brick buildings replaced the simpler wooden buildings of the port's early days. But when the railroad failed to materialize, Port Townsend's building boom collapsed. So sudden was the bust that some of the grand, multistory brick commercial blocks along Water Street never had the interiors of their upper floors completed. By the depression of 1893, a city built for twenty thousand was left with a population of two thousand.

The development of nearby Fort Worden to protect the entrance to Puget Sound brought temporary prosperity during World War I. Peace, however, led to another decline in the local economy. Lumbering and wood processing was the one industry that stayed; in 1928 a mill was built outside the town that continues as the area's single largest employer.

Expectations of riches had created Port Townsend, but poverty preserved what survived of it. The great county courthouse of 1892 (still in use) and the large Customs House of 1893 (now the post office) stand as reminders of hopes never realized. The commercial

An iron safe made in Ohio sits in the hallway of the Jefferson County Courthouse.

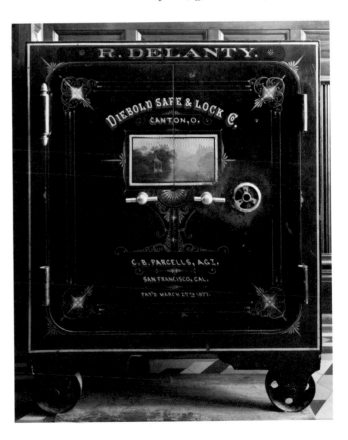

Expectations that Port Townsend would become the terminus of the railroad led to a frantic building boom in 1889. The rear corner of the block of Water Street between Taylor and Tyler (now a parking lot), seen from the bluff above the commercial district, was never completed after the railroad changed its plans.

This massive red-brick commercial building of 1889 has recently been reborn as the Palace Hotel.

district along Water Street saw its streetcar tracks pulled up as the town contracted. Great Victorian houses were abandoned to the county from failure to pay property taxes.

Eventually the town stabilized, and local commerce, the nearby lumber mill, and the reduced army post kept the town alive. No money existed for the wholesale façade "improvements" that disfigured so many other small cities. The logical future for Port Townsend—now that its rarity is appreciated by both residents and visitors—is tourism. Ferry boats from Seattle operate during the summer months, and the state arts commission runs a variety of arts and recreation programs at Fort Worden.

But all is not perfect here, despite the generally positive attitudes of many in Port Townsend toward their heritage. The new shopping center on the road leading into Port Townsend's downtown can only serve to drain commerce away, and the seasonal tourist industry cannot really take up all the slack. Restoring the big old brick buildings is expensive, and there is no market for their upper-story spaces. In the past such unused spaces would have become low-rent living units or even artists' studios, but it is far too expensive to bring these buildings up to modern codes. In addition, overactive real estate speculation has driven up the prices of old buildings beyond the realistic income of a small shop or hotel operator.

Because of the Water Street Historic District's rarity as an example of a late-Victorian commercial district with few modern intrusions, the National Trust for Historic Preservation, with a grant from the Architecture and Environmental Arts Program of the National Endowment for the Arts, conducted a thor-

The turreted Queen Anne–style Frank W. Hastings house was built in 1890. Because of the town's sudden bust, its interior remained unfinished for another fourteen years. Today it has been refurbished and serves the town's new tourist industry as a bed-and-breakfast inn.

ough planning study of the area. Among its recommendations was restricting the amount of undeveloped land zoned for commercial use, to prevent new development from draining away the businesses in the old downtown. Such recommendations are politically difficult, if not impossible, since even towns aware of their historic qualities tend to believe that more growth is always good. Many consider down-zoning confiscatory, while all local special interests, from those who own just one undeveloped lot to major industries, continually press for special treatment for their holdings. All too often the common good is sacrificed to benefit politically well-connected developers. A rich architectural heritage is not enough: there must be a sound economic base and the political will of the community to shape its future.

The Peter Mutty house at Taylor and Lawrence streets was built in 1891 and has been continuously cherished ever since. The original cast-iron cresting atop its roof and porch is an extraordinary survival.

Fort Worden's officers' row preserves an outstanding collection of colonial revival upper-middle-class houses. The house on the left was the commanding officer's. The post has been preserved by the Washington State Parks and Recreation Commission as a conference and arts center.

AMERICAN MILITARY HERITAGE

The Puget Sound and Columbia River Forts, Washington

AMONG THE most important institutions in the development of the American West was the U.S. Army, which first secured the hostile Indian territory in the interior and later built extensive coastal fortifications. In the nineteenth century these installations were in or near cities. Along with the massive subsidies given to privately owned railroads, army and navy installations were the principal tool by which the national government spurred the economic development of the West before the huge irrigation projects of this century. Then as now, military spending was a critical catalyst in local economies.

Though adapted to local climatic conditions, these facilities were designed back East, and they represent national architectural styles in an especially pure form. Designed and built to last, fitted into their landscapes on spacious reservations, insulated from taxation or commercial pressures to turn a profit, and immune from passing fashions and misimprovements, the chief military installations are perhaps the West's most important repositories of America's national architectural heritage. Until recently they were especially well maintained. Today the army is the first federal entity to comply with Congressional mandates to properly inventory its architectural heritage.

Such has been the gap between weapons development and architecture that the more ambitious of these installations were technically obsolete the day their first brick was laid. Fort Point in San Francisco, begun in 1854 on the Golden Gate, had been made

The functionally placed windows on the sidewall of one of the houses on Fort Worden's officers' row, built in 1904–1905, create a striking abstract pattern.

obsolete by new developments in masonry-piercing naval guns before it was garrisoned in 1861. Yet, though the United States' first line of defense in the nineteenth century was its navy, fortifications continued to be built well into the twentieth century.

By the time of World War I, economic considerations became increasingly important in the placement of military installations. Because costs were higher and disciplinary problems were more acute in and near large cities, the armed services shifted their larger operations to remote rural areas. This made old urban bases obsolete.

As historic posts became redundant these spacious facilities were turned over to the National Park Service, as at Fort Mason in San Francisco, or to state governments, the most responsible and imaginative of which has been Washington. When Fort Worden, near Port Townsend, became redundant it was converted into the state's Juvenile Treatment Center in 1957. In 1972 the Washington State Parks and Recreation Commission took over the historic fort and converted it into conference facilities and vacation housing. The Fort Worden Conference and Cultural Arts Center then created the Centrum Foundation, which has attracted many artists, dancers, and musicians for workshops, professional symposia, and public performances. Visitors may camp on the grounds or stay overnight in the old barracks, since converted into hostels. Art, poetry, music, dance, and crafts now flourish where soldiers once paraded.

Across the parade ground from officers' row is the post's headquarters, built in 1908, flanked by the enlisted mens' barracks of 1904, each of which housed 109 soldiers. Stylistically conservative, these buildings represent the epitome of American wooden vernacular architecture as it evolved during the nineteenth century.

It seems legitimate to quibble, however, with the decision to paint the once-uniform officers' row a variety of different colors. Relying on the same color is how these varied buildings, from headquarters to storage sheds, were brought together in the military landscape. Uniformity is central to military architecture and dress. It is also how these complexes differed from the civilian landscape. To change this, even to the mild colors that have been chosen, is to change an essential part of this historic environment.

Seen from the porch of the enlisted men's barracks is Battery Ord, an eight-inch gun battery whose ordnance has long been removed. It was completed in 1898 to guard the entrance to the Columbia River. It never fired a hostile shot and has been preserved as a monument to the coast defenses of the period.

The enlisted men's barracks at Fort Worden was built to standard Army plans in 1902 and is a classic piece of American design. It has been restored, painted white and green, and serves as the interpretive center for this state park.

AFTER THE MALL: REINVESTMENT IN AN OLD INDUSTRIAL CITY

Tacoma, Washington

THE Interstate Highway Act of 1956 has done more to change the American landscape than anything since the coming of the railroads in the nineteenth century. The massive shifts that occurred as industry moved out to larger, cheaper tracts where new, one-story plants could be built drained away both jobs and the tax base from old industrial and urban centers. When suburbanization followed the new highways, the commercial functions of old city cores moved out to new highway-oriented shopping centers. Downtowns rapidly declined; poverty increased in old centers; and high taxes and the "prudent" policies of banks and lending institutions that redlined old districts prevented normal reinvestment in established centers. The best architectural works of the nineteenth century, usually in the center of the old downtown, often languished underutilized or were abandoned. The collective investments of a century began to crumble.

The solution that emerged was as drastic as the problem: the malling of main street and the demolition of most of its flanking blocks for parking lots.

Outdoor advertising is a particularly American element in the landscape, but not all appreciate even the best examples of it. This fine two-story-high advertisement for a local brewery depicted Mount Rainier in purple and white but was painted over when the Massasoit Hotel of 1888 was restored in 1982.

A front view of the hotel, in Tacoma's Union Depot/Warehouse Historic District, undergoing restoration.

(Opposite): The Italian Renaissance–style old Tacoma City Hall, designed by San Francisco architects Hatherton and McIntosh in 1893, is built of fine yellow Roman brick with terra-cotta ornament. Vacated by the city in 1959, it stood empty until its adaptation into offices in 1972. Today it is the center of the Old City Hall Historic District.

Tacoma's Broadway was malled in the 1960s and large public expenditures were made for paving, canopies, fountains, and other amenities. But while public powers could impose sign control, nothing could be done to force private property owners to restore the façades of previously misimproved buildings.

Today, after the mall, efforts are being made to design modern shop fronts compatible with old buildings. Weyerhaeuser's Cornerstone Development Company's Tacoma office in the 1905 Knights of Pythias Building on the Broadway mall epitomizes this new awareness.

Fine buildings were ripped down, once coherent cities were torn apart, inner-city deserts were created. The result was only a further shrinking of taxable property, as fewer profitable enterprises were forced to carry larger municipal debts. The irony of these new malled streets was that in aiming to serve the car-borne shopper, they closed their main shopping street to the normal flow of traffic and thereby stopped the natural process whereby shoppers passing a store might drop in to buy on impulse. Pedestrianizing main street at the same time that shoppers

stopped walking struck no one as illogical. Cities such as Spokane, San Francisco, and Santa Barbara—all of which resisted this deadly solution—have done better in retaining both their downtown retail activity and their architectural heritage than places such as Yuma, Sacramento, and Tacoma, which malled their principal shopping streets.

The problem has now become what to do with the nineteenth-century main streets that have been malled. So far few cities have torn out the over-designed promenades installed in the former road-

The industrial district south of Tacoma's downtown is undergoing adaptive reuse and architectural restoration. The early converters are often architects, engineers, or contract furniture showrooms. Once a former red-brick industrial district is completely rehabilitated, higher-rent uses such as law or advertising offices can be expected to follow.

The unexpectedly elegant, templelike Puget Sound Power and Light substation in Tacoma's Union Depot/Warehouse Historic District is an early, if crude, example of adaptive reuse: it serves as a tire recapping plant.

Northern Pacific Railroad's headquarters building was designed by Charles B. Talbot and built in 1888 on a bluff at the northern end of the business district. Now part of the Old City Hall Historic District, the building has been restored as first-class office space since this photo was taken.

bed and allowed cars to return to their normal circulation patterns. Instead, malled main streets in "progressive" cities are trying to make themselves over into downtown shopping centers, usually by constructing large new hotels and office complexes immediately adjacent to turn-of-the-century streets turned into 1960s malls. However, the big department stores—the real engines of lively retail districts —have yet to reverse their shift to areas in the outer ring beyond the traditional suburbs.

Downtown Tacoma exemplifies the dilemma of what to do "after the mall." It developed as a major city because of the decision of the Northern Pacific Railroad to make Tacoma its Puget Sound terminus in 1873. Equally important for Tacoma in the long run was the railroad's inducing St. Paul, Minnesota, lumberman Frederic Weyerhaeuser to buy vast tracts of railroad-owned timber lands in the Northwest; for while the railroad's economic importance has declined, Weyerhaeuser's trees have continued growing. But the Minnesota lumber baron chose not to fell his Northwest timber right away. "Not for ourselves, not for our children, but for our grandchildren," said Weyerhaeuser of his Western forest holdings. Tacoma became the headquarters of this giant forest-product company, its offices scattered throughout the downtown. Finally it, too, suburbanized to a new corporate headquarters, one of the finest modern buildings in the Northwest, built in 1971 on the interstate highway between Tacoma and

Designed by architects Reed and Stem and opened in 1911, Tacoma's grand Union Station, with its green, copper-clad dome, is the anchor of the Union Depot/Warehouse Historic District. It is a measure of the success of the preservation movement that the building will most certainly not be demolished, though it now stands empty and its future use is unknown.

Seattle. Downtown Tacoma's last economic prop collapsed with the departure of its richest corporation.

But unlike so many companies that have abandoned the inner city, Weyerhaeuser—perhaps be-

While reinvestment is reviving Tacoma's brick buildings, its great wooden buildings may soon disappear completely—a great irony in a region whose most important industry is lumbering. Here the old Tacoma Municipal Dock, with its great green shed and expressive heavy-timber portal, awaits reuse.

cause of its consciously long-range point of view in the management of its forests—decided to apply the same approach to urban real estate. In 1979 Cornerstone Development Company, a subsidiary of Weyerhaeuser Real Estate, was formed to develop large-scale, mixed-use projects in historic downtown areas. Both Seattle, the dominant metropolis in today's Northwest, and Tacoma have benefited from the decision to make massive reinvestments in old cores. Unlike so many large-scale capital investments in older areas where everything already standing is cleared away for high-rise development, Cornerstone set out to rehabilitate older buildings as a complement to its plans for new construction.

In downtown Tacoma, Cornerstone's investments are reshaping the stillborn Broadway mall (here known as a plaza). The fundamental problem, now that urban renewal has surrounded the old main street with big new parking lots and garages, was bringing in business and people. The current solution is to build a large new first-class, twenty-two-story hotel and the tallest office tower in the city right next to the Broadway Plaza. A block away (with a parking garage intervening) will be a new YMCA athletic facility. Along Broadway's mall several historic buildings are being restored to create new, upscale retail facilities. Finally, at the head of the mall, B. Marcus Priteca's ornate Pantages Theater of 1918 has already been restored by the city of Tacoma to serve as a performing-arts center to bring people into the downtown at night. Perhaps no large city in the West is experiencing such an ambitious revitalization as downtown Tacoma, principally due to great infusions of capital by both taxpayers and home-town business interests.

While still in use, the Canadian Cedar Company's mustard-colored mill on East D Street on Tacoma's city waterway is only minimally maintained. Such local vernacular structures are not considered "historic" and are vanishing one by one due to fire or neglect.

Designed by J. F. Everett, Seattle's Pioneer Square Pergola, a cast-iron and glass shelter for trolley and cable car passengers, was built in 1909. Now in the heart of the Pioneer Square Historic District, this singular amenity was restored in 1970 with a grant from the United Parcel Service, commemorating its founding in Seattle.

PRESERVATION LEADER IN THE WEST

Seattle, Washington

GIVEN Seattle's outstanding record in architectural preservation and urban conservation, it is ironic that the phrase "Skid Row" should be the city's most notable contribution to our language. The original Skid Road (not Row), now known as Yesler Way, bisects the Pioneer Square Historic District. The street was named after the logs that were skidded down the originally forested slopes to Henry Yesler's sawmill on Puget Sound's Elliott Bay. The frame settlement that stood here was wiped away by a great fire in 1889. When the city rebuilt, it used brick and stone instead. The railroads that linked Seattle and Spokane with Minneapolis and St. Paul, and beyond them with Chicago, brought the contemporary com-

The post-1889 brick buildings along First Avenue in Pioneer Square have all been carefully restored; simply designed sidewalk cafés add life to the streets.

Elmer H. Fisher's landmark Pioneer Building of 1889–1890 facing triangular Pioneer Square Park was Seattle's most prestigious address at the time of the Klondike Gold Rush of 1897–1898. Forgotten as modern Seattle's business district shifted northward, it was restored in 1973–1974.

The fine Chicago School Maynard Building of 1892 was restored by Olson/Walker Architects in 1974. This compatible sign proudly records its rebirth.

While brick and stone characterize the new city that rose from the ashes of the great fire of 1889, fanciful metal work accents the Pioneer Square Historic District in everything from railings to the elegant Pergola of 1909.

mercial architecture of the firm of Burnham and Root as well as others of the Chicago School to the Pacific Northwest. One outstanding architect, Elmer H. Fisher, left an indelible stamp on the rebuilt city in many fine designs. The city boomed in 1897–1898 as the gateway to the Yukon Gold Rush.

But despite large investments, such as the Smith Tower of 1914, Seattle's downtown shifted north, discarding the old brick city. By World War I Skid Road had acquired its contemporary meaning. But the flophouses and cheap bars that took over the area meant its eventual preservation as well. Although a downtown plan in the late 1950s proposed wiping away both blight and history, and the piecemeal destruction of the district seemed imminent when two historic hotels were torn down in 1960 to construct a parking garage, Seattle preservationists fought the idea and the area became the city's first historic district, Pioneer Square. Private investors bought the handsome brick buildings back to life with shops, restaurants, bars, theaters, art galleries, and refurbished offices. Eventually the National Park Service established a part of its Klondike Gold Rush Historic Park in this area, which had outfitted the miners.

Seattle's other early preservation battle was over the future of the colorful Pike Place Market, established in 1907, when the mayor proclaimed the street space of Pike Place a market where farmers could sell their produce directly to the public. Soon permanent buildings were constructed along the street with shops, housing, and offices; ultimately, market stalls within the buildings replaced the produce wagons. But by the 1960s the market had fallen on hard times and it, like Pioneer Square, fit the urban-renewal planners' definition of blight. Archi-

The gleaming white, terra-cotta-clad steel-frame Smith Tower of 1914 was built by typewriter tycoon L. C. Smith, with the intention of anchoring Seattle's downtown in the Pioneer Square area. But the downtown shifted northward nevertheless. After years of neglect, the landmark skyscraper was purchased by Seattle restaurateur Ivar Haglund, who restored it using state grants. An antique elevator cab still carries visitors to its observation deck.

(Above): Preservation in Seattle has affected more than just Pioneer Square. Weyerhaeuser's Cornerstone Development Company is restoring and building on six square blocks of waterfront property adjacent to the downtown. Here the Alexis Hotel undergoes extensive rehabilitation.

(Right): Partial preservation in Seattle's Waterfront Place includes the terra-cotta entrance to this 1915 building.

tect Victor Steinbrueck led the Friends of the Market to agitate for its preservation. In 1971 city·voters passed an initiative to establish a seven-acre historic district, in order to protect the market and prevent its destruction. Preservation—in this case the preservation of a utilitarian district devoid of high architecture—proved its political strength among the people of Seattle. The primary goal of the historic district is the preservation of the market function; a twelve-member citizen commission oversees changes in use as well as design. Concurrent changes in federal policy fortunately allowed urban-renewal funds to finance not the district's replacement but its rehabilitation. Protective covenants on property held and managed by a nonprofit public development authority are part of this redevelopment project. Today, with its stalls, restaurants, and residences, the Pike Place Market is one of the liveliest places in Seattle, drawing both residents and visitors to its smells, sounds, tastes, and visual delights.

During the 1970s Seattle emerged as one of the most imaginative preservation-minded cities in the nation. The Historic Seattle Preservation and Development Authority was created by the city and ini-

The new Watermark Tower Building recycles the ground floor façade of a 1915 structure in a high-rise.

As in San Francisco, an elevated freeway has cut off the city from its waterfront. To preserve and revive it, Seattle has recently installed a waterfront streetcar, using 1927 rolling stock from Melbourne, Australia. The line links Pioneer Square with the ferry terminal and lively Pike Place Market.

tially funded with $600,000 in federal revenue-sharing money. These funds allowed the nonprofit authority to buy and restore historic buildings, both commercial and residential. Federal loan programs were directed toward the restoration of historic residences. Seattle also diligently sought out federal money for matching grants under the National Historic Preservation Act of 1966. A combination of public and private investment, plus political leadership provided by Mayor Wesley C. Uhlman, transformed the city. Preservation emerged as a citywide movement that took hold not only in historic commercial districts but in the city's varied neighborhoods as well. Today, while federal money for historic preservation has all but dried up, private investment in older buildings continues. In everything from individual houses to the Cornerstone Development Company's six-block restoration-and-new-construction Waterfront Place project, Seattle continues to build on its successes. Architectural preservation, along with strong public interest in natural conservation, is a key part of what has made Seattle, now the Pacific Northwest's largest city, one of the most livable big cities in the nation.

Across Lake Union from Seattle's high-rises is one of the most imaginative preservation projects in the West. Gas Works Park was created in 1978 from an obsolete turn-of-the-century plant, a monument of the "smokestack" industrial age. (Opposite): The old compressor building is now a play barn. (Left): An imaginative ground-level sundial by Charles Greening brings art to this once-workaday landscape.

Seattle has preserved its domestic architectural heritage. Architect Ellsworth Storey's designs of the early 1900s blended the Craftsman aesthetic with local materials such as red-cedar shingles to create a classic regional architecture.

Outside the small town of Spangle stands this traditional clapboard, gambrel-roofed horse-and-mule barn, which is gently falling into ruin.

THE PASSING OF THE REGIONAL BARN

Spangle and Oysterville, Washington

THERE ARE many ironies in architectural preservation, perhaps the bitterest being that those buildings least American—rich men's châteaux, Gothic churches—are those most often preserved. On the other hand, those structures more intimately connected with the nation's development—mines, mills, and barns—are the least loved and the first cleared away when they have outlived their usefulness, despite the fact that these structures are often so much more interesting than the "high art" monuments derived from European designs.

In the Northwest, with influences and antecedents

This farmstead in the rich Palouse wheatland of eastern Washington shows the changes in the modern farm landscape. To the right of the farmhouse with its man-planted trees stand a great traditional barn with its successor, the much simpler modern prefabricated metal structure.

from the Midwest, the East, and Central Europe, especially handsome, swelling barn forms were created. In the Palouse Hills, the great wheat belt of eastern Washington, where the land is abundantly productive but the winters are harsh, the West saw its greatest barn-building. The West's farms have always stressed machinery and technology. Before mechanized equipment, horses and mules propelled the combines that plowed, planted, cultivated, and reaped. Mules and horses had to be housed and fed over the long winters, and great barns were built with the animals downstairs and their feed stored above.

From practical necessity came beautiful structures. For while the houses of the prosperous farm owners were but simpler versions of what rich urbanites were building in tree-shaded suburbs, the barns of the Northwest are vernacular architectural creations of the greatest importance. Big, simple, devoid of ornament, the gambrel-roofed barns of Washington State are major monuments on the American rural landscape.

But the force that called them forth—a highly capitalized agricultural technology—is the force that has moved beyond them, making them obsolete, too expensive to maintain, and, eventually, only a memory on the rolling, wheat-rich land. Today's diesel-powered farms have no need for great two-story barns. One-story, prefabricated metal sheds are enough to house the machines that are silent at night. The very same corrugated-metal sheds that serve in industrial districts serve just as well on farms.

While farmers now build new sheds to house their expensive mechanical equipment, they generally do not tear down the great, swelling barns their fathers built. They use them for storage, defer painting them, and let them slowly fall into ruin. Eventually a great wind or severe storm accomplishes the demolition that the farmers themselves were so reluctant to do. With every winter, more of the American indigenous architectural heritage vanishes.

The exterior and interior of a shingled gambrel-roofed barn in coastal Oysterville, now unused, epitomize the traditional local barn. The curved rafters of the roof are made from five laminated boards bolted together. The flared edges of the roof protect vents that prevented the hay stored upstairs from spoiling.

After Expo '74, the 1909 carousel from a demolished amusement park was reerected in the new River Front Park.

When Spokane redeveloped its riverfront for Expo '74, both the unsightly railyards and, unfortunately, the Great Northern Railroad Depot of 1902 were cleared away. The depot's stately campanile alone was preserved, its musical chimes a happy link with the past.

PRESERVING JOY IN THE CITY

Spokane, Washington

ONE OF the greatest architectural and preservation surprises in the West is Spokane, self-proclaimed capital of an "inland empire." Deep in the interior of eastern Washington, and with strong historical links to Minneapolis and St. Paul, Spokane is the greatest exception to the seeming rule that coastal Western cities take better care of their urban heritage than inland places. While there has been demolition and loss in Spokane, both in its downtown and in its inner-city residential areas, there has been an equally strong determination to keep the center alive and to preserve the commercial base of the downtown, not just in offices but in stores, amusements, and restaurants as well.

The arrival of the Northern Pacific Railroad in 1881 and soon thereafter the Union Pacific, the Great Northern, and the Chicago–Milwaukee–St. Paul and Pacific made Spokane a great railroad center in the West. Situated on the falls of the Spokane River, which were harnessed early for electric power, the city blossomed further with the discovery of gold and silver in nearby Idaho's Coeur d'Alene district in 1883. Spokane became the main supply point for prospectors headed toward the mines and, eventually, the home for those lucky few whose expectations were fulfilled. When a great fire wiped out

the city in 1889, Spokane had the money and the will to rebuild handsomely.

Most important in the long run was the fact that Spokane was far enough away from other centers,

Adopting an idea from Minneapolis and St. Paul, Spokane has kept its downtown alive by linking together many of its new and old office buildings and department stores with enclosed pedestrian bridges, which are in turn connected to two huge parking garages.

either Minneapolis and St. Paul to the east, or Seattle, Portland, or San Francisco on the coast, to be free to dominate a vast region. The money from the mines in Idaho and later in British Columbia was not drained away, and Spokane developed its own elite with strong ties to their city. When the region to the south began to exploit its rich soil, creating one of the greatest wheat-growing regions in North America, that wealth, too, came to Spokane. In the colorful Kirtland Kelsey Cutter and the autodidact Willis A. Ritchie, among others, the city found architects worthy of its purses in the heady 1880s.

In the nineteenth century the all-powerful railroads commandeered the city's scenic riverfront for railyards and terminals, and trapped the downtown in an iron vise of massive elevated tracks. Resented in the railroad era, these tracks nevertheless had a

The Bennett Block was built in 1890, one year after Spokane's great fire. Its ground floor has been remodeled, a skywalk connection made with a central parking garage, and a modern glassed-in elevator built behind it linking it with more parking.

In the restored Bennett Block, planters echo the florid cast iron of the piers between the shop fronts. (Far right): Evidence of the building's checkered past remains in unrestored touches such as this chipped stonework.

salutary long-term effect: they forced the downtown area to stay put, so that the city kept its central focus. When the railyards on the river were torn away to make room for Expo '74, the downtown finally faced its greatest natural feature, Spokane Falls, and broke out to create the lively River Front Park, complete with a restored 1909 carousel that had been saved when the Natatorium amusement park was demolished in 1968. Many contemporary high-rises have, alas, displaced good buildings of the post-1889 era of reconstruction, but many others have been saved.

In the nineteenth century the city looked to the East—whence its principal railroads came—for its architectural styles. In the twentieth century, the same thing happened: in the 1960s, Spokane looked to Minneapolis and St. Paul, where a system of second-story pedestrian bridges was being built to

A contemporary in-fill building on the same block as the Bennett Block and across the street from the central parking garage might be mistaken for a historic building, even though it is brand-new. While not literally a Victorian design, this downtown restaurant does capture the whimsy of the period's house designs.

The Riverside Avenue Historic District, immediately west of the downtown, is a remarkably direct expression of the coherence of Spokane's civic leadership. To the left is the 1919 Elks Club, now adapted to offices; to the right, the colonnaded Masonic Temple of 1905 and 1925.

Beyond is the arcaded Renaissance revival Chamber of Commerce of 1933, and behind it, the red and white Spokane Club of 1910, designed by Cutter and Malmgren. This "power row" is still the business and social epicenter of the "inland empire."

Architect Chauncey Seaton's exclamatory
Spokesman-Review *Building of 1891 is perhaps the
finest Romanesque revival monument in the West, still
occupied by the newspaper that built it. With its tower
illuminated at night, it is a splendid ornament to the
Spokane skyline. A new wing is being added; meanwhile,
the original marble-and-bronze entrance remains intact.*

make the downtown more livable during the winter. Spokane took this idea, and, in its more compact downtown, has created the most extensive such pedestrian system in the nation. Connected to a huge parking garage near the center of the city, this ar-

The Clark Mansion of 1898, designed by Spokane's most colorful architect, Kirtland Kelsey Cutter, fuses a wildly eclectic exterior with everything from fashionable French to exotic Moorish interiors. After serving as a mansion, inn, and private museum, it is now a luxury restaurant.

rangement has satisfied both the modern American's devotion to private transportation and provided the comfort of controlled "public spaces." Not always felicitous when such "skywalks" crash into the second story of nineteenth-century buildings obviously not designed for them, these bridges (and the garage they are connected with) have nonetheless kept the downtown attractive to the middle class. While this solution is not applicable in most cities, it has worked in Spokane and has helped preserve joy in one city.

The Coeur d'Alene Park across the street from the Clark Mansion was named after the Idaho silver bonanza that put Spokane on the map. A landscape jewel only now at the peak of maturation, it mixes tall native pines with shorter, exotic trees. Parks are often as man-made as buildings, but only in the last few years has their conservation emerged as a recognized dimension of preservation.

PRESERVING JOY IN THE CITY 175

REGIONAL SOURCE GUIDE

National Trust for Historic Preservation

National Trust for Historic Preservation
1785 Massachusetts Avenue, N.W.
Washington, D.C. 20036
(202) 673-4000

National Trust for Historic Preservation
Western Regional Office
1 Sutter Street
San Francisco, California 94104
(415) 974-8420

State Historic Preservation Offices and Key Regional Research Libraries

Arizona

Historic Preservation Officer
Arizona State Parks
1688 West Adams
Phoenix, Arizona 85007
(602) 255-4174

Arizona Historical Society and Library
949 East Second Street
Tucson, Arizona 85719
(602) 882-5774

Heritage Foundation of Arizona
Box 25616
Tempe, Arizona 85282
(602) 627-2773

California

State Historic Preservation Officer
Department of Parks and Recreation
State Resources Agency
1220 K Street
Sacramento, California 95811
(916) 445-8006

Bancroft Library
University of California, Berkeley
Berkeley, California 94720
(415) 642-6481

California Historical Society History Center
6300 Wilshire Boulevard
Los Angeles, California 90048
(213) 651-5655

California Historical Society Library
2099 Pacific Avenue
San Francisco, California 94109
(415) 567-1848

California Preservation Foundation
55 Sutter Street, Suite 593
San Francisco, California 94109
(415) 527-7808

San Diego Historical Society Library
Serra Museum, 2727 Presidio Drive
San Diego, California 92138
(619) 297-3258

Idaho

State Historic Preservation Officer
Idaho Historical Society
610 North Julia Davis Drive
Boise, Idaho 83702
(208) 334-2120

Idaho State Historical Society Library
325 West State Street
Boise, Idaho 83702
(208) 384-3356

Idaho Historic Preservation Council
   Box 1495
   Boise, Idaho 83701
   (208) 334-2120

Nevada

State Historic Preservation Officer
Department of Conservation and Natural Resources
   201 South Fall Street, Room 113
   Carson City, Nevada 89710
   (702) 885-5138

Nevada Historical Society Library
   1650 North Virginia Street
   Reno, Nevada 89503
   (702) 784-6397

Oregon

State Historic Preservation Officer
State Parks Superintendent
   525 Trade Street, S.E.
   Salem, Oregon 97310
   (503) 378-5002

Historic Preservation League of Oregon
   Box 40053
   Portland, Oregon 97240
   (503) 243-1923

Oregon Historical Society Library
   1230 S.W. Park Avenue
   Portland, Oregon 97205
   (503) 222-1741

Utah

State Historic Preservation Officer
Utah State Historical Society

   300 Rio Grande
   Salt Lake City, Utah 84101
   (801) 533-7039

Utah Heritage Foundation
   355 Quince Street
   Salt Lake City, Utah 84103
   (801) 533-0858

Washington

State Historic Preservation Officer
Office of Archaeology and Historic Preservation
   111 West Twenty-first Avenue, KL-11
   Olympia, Washington 98504
   (206) 753-4117

University of Washington Library
   Special Collections
   Seattle, Washington 98195
   (206) 593-2830

Washington State Historical Society Library
   315 North Stadium Way
   Tacoma, Washington 98403
   (206) 593-2830

Washington Trust for Historic Preservation
   111 West Twenty-first Avenue
   Olympia, Washington 89501
   (206) 573-0099

General Works

Bartlett, Richard A. *The New Country: A Social History of the American Frontier, 1776–1890.* New York: Oxford University Press, 1974.

Johnson, Paul C., and Dorothy Krell, eds. *The California Missions: A Pictorial History.* Menlo Park, Calif.: Sunset Books, 1979.

Maddex, Diane, ed. *All About Old Buildings: The Whole Preservation Catalog.* Washington, D.C.: Preservation Press, 1985.

Meinig, D. W. *The Southwest: Three Peoples in Geographical Change, 1600–1970.* New York: Oxford University Press, 1971.

National Trust for Historic Preservation, Tony P. Wrenn, and Elizabeth D. Mulloy. *America's Forgotten Architecture.* Washington, D.C.: Preservation Press, 1985.

Reps, John W. *Cities of the American West: A History of Frontier Urban Planning.* Princeton, N.J.: Princeton University Press, 1979. (Numerous maps and views.)

State Guidebooks Old and New

Arizona

Federal Writers' Project, Works Progress Administration. *Arizona: A State Guide.* American Guide Series. New York: Hastings House, 1940.

Giebner, Robert C., ed. *Tucson Preservation Primer: A Guide for the Property Owner.* Tucson: University of Arizona Press, 1981.

California

Corbett, Michael R. *Splendid Survivors: San Francisco's Downtown Architectural Heritage.* San Francisco: California Living Books, 1979.

Delahanty, Randolph. *California: A Guidebook.* San Diego: Harcourt Brace Jovanovich, 1984.

———. *San Francisco: Walks and Tours in the Golden Gate City.* New York: Dial Press, 1980.

Federal Writers' Project, Works Progress Administration. *California: A Guide to the Golden State.* American Guide Series. New York: Hastings House, 1939. (Reissued 1983 by Pantheon Books, New York, as *The WPA Guide to California.*)

———. *Los Angeles: A Guide to the City and Its Environs.* American Guide Series. New York: Hastings House, 1941.

———. *San Francisco: The Bay and Its Cities.* American Guide Series. New York: Hastings House, 1940.

Gebhard, David, Roger Montgomery, Robert Winter, John Woodbridge, and Sally Woodbridge. *A Guide to Architecture in San Francisco and Northern California.* 2d ed. Salt Lake City: Peregrine Smith, 1976.

Gebhard, David, and Robert Winter. *A Guide to Architecture in Los Angeles and Southern California.* Salt Lake City: Peregrine Smith, 1977.

Idaho

Federal Writers' Project, Works Progress Administration. *Idaho: A Guide in Word and Picture.*

American Guide Series. Caldwell, Idaho: The Caxton Printers, 1937.

Nevada

Federal Writers' Project, Works Progress Administration. *Nevada: A Guide to the Silver State.* American Guide Series. Portland: Binfords & Mort, 1940.

Oregon

Clarke, Rosalind. *Architecture Oregon Style: A Photographic History of Architecture in the West.* Albany, Oregon: City of Albany, 1983.

Federal Writers' Project, Works Progress Administration. *Oregon: The End of the Trail.* Rev. ed. American Guide Series. Portland: Binsford & Mort, 1951.

Vaughn, Thomas, ed. *Space, Style, and Structure: Oregon and Washington Architecture.* Seattle: University of Washington Press, 1980.

Utah

Federal Writers' Project, Works Progress Administration. *Utah: A Guide to the State.* American Guide Series. New York: Hastings House, 1941.

Washington

Federal Writers' Project, Works Progress Administration. *The New Washington: A Guide to the Evergreen State.* Rev. ed. Portland: Washington State Historical Society, 1950.

Woodbridge, Sally B., and Roger Montgomery. *A Guide to Architecture in Washington State: An Environmental Perspective.* Seattle: University of Washington Press, 1980.

Architectural Style Guides

Blumenson, John J.-G. *Identifying American Architecture: A Pictorial Guide to Styles and Terms, 1600–1945.* Nashville, Tenn.: American Association for State and Local History, 1977. (Good for building terms.)

Poppeliers, John, S. Allen Chambers, Nancy B. Schwartz, Historic American Buildings Survey. *What Style Is It? A Guide to American Architecture* (1977). Rev. ed. Washington, D.C.: Preservation Press, 1984.

Whiffen, Marcus. *American Architecture Since 1780: A Guide to the Styles.* Cambridge, Mass.: M.I.T. Press, 1981. (Best guide to the styles.)

RANDOLPH DELAHANTY, born in Memphis, Tennessee, in 1944, grew up in New Jersey. He holds degrees in history from Georgetown, Chicago, and Harvard, and is a historian, city-planning consultant, architectural restoration specialist, and lecturer. He has written guides to California and to San Francisco, where he lives, and is working on a historical and landscape guide to the United States.

E. ANDREW MCKINNEY was born in Eugene, Oregon, in 1945, and studied anthropology at Portland State College. He has lived in San Francisco since 1967, where he is an architectural and product photographer. He has done extensive scenic photography throughout the western United States, especially in the national parks.

RANDOLPH LANGENBACH was born in Boston in 1945, and studied architecture at Harvard College. A graduate of Harvard's Graduate School of Design, he has practiced as a consultant in building conservation and preservation planning. As an architectural photographer, he has concentrated on industrial structures in New England, England, and India. He is a professor of architecture at the University of California, Berkeley.